Avoiding the Retirement Trap

fifty profiles of people from
every state in the union
who are doing something meaningful with
their
retirement

by Virginia Robinson French
photographs by James C. French

ACTA Publications
Chicago, Illinois

Avoiding the Retirement Trap
fifty profiles of people from every state in the
union who are doing something meaningful
with their retirement

by Virginia Robinson French
photographs by James C. French

Ginny French is a former school teacher and Jim
French a former engineer for WGN radio and television in Chicago. They raised eight children of their
own and have thirteen grandchildren. The Frenches
live near Dundee, Illinois (when they are not traveling somewhere else).

Edited by Gregory F. Augustine Pierce
Artwork by Isz
Typesetting by Garrison Publications

Copyright © 1994 by   ACTA Publications
4848 N. Clark Street
Chicago, IL 60640
312-271030

Year 99 98 97 96 95 94

Printing 6 5 4 3 2 1

ISBN: 0-87946-095-4

Library of Congress Number: 94-072526

Printed in the United States of America

CONTENTS

DEDICATION

This book is dedicated to our big bunch of grown-up children who spurred us on, mile by mile and page by page. We also acknowledge the wonderful people across the country who shared their lives and hospitality with us during our fun adventure.

Ginny and Jim French

"... live all the days of your life."
Polite Conversation, Jonathan Swift

FOREWORD

We had long suspected that retirement is like a yawning net, ensnaring many persons who no longer work for a living and holding them captive—immobile, ineffectual, and without dignity. We blithely called it "the retirement trap."

Then one day it suddenly occurred to us that we too are approaching the danger zone surrounding the trap, just as you are, whatever your age or career status. You. Your husband. Your wife. Your boss. Your co-workers. Your parents. Your friends. Even your adult children.

Unless we die very young, each of us must one day face the challenging after-years and make a conscious choice. Entrapment? Or freedom and fulfillment?

This book is about the retirement trap and the people we discovered all over the United States who managed to elude it.

It is our hope that after you meet the persons on the pages ahead, you will follow their example, waltz lightly around the trap, and live happily ever after.

THE BEGINNING

We were high above the Atlantic flying home from Puerto Rico when the idea struck.

A few years before, Jim and I had resigned from our respective careers. You will note that we did not "retire," no matter what they call it in the Illinois Teachers' Pension Office, the Social Security Headquarters, or the Department in Charge of Former Employees of WGN Radio and Television in Chicago. We *know* what we did! *We resigned!*

After all, we have our mental health to consider and we both become acutely violent when identified with the words "retired," "retiree," "senior citizen," "Aging American" (upper or lower case), "old," "graying American," "the geriatric group," "golden agers," "gray panthers," or "blue hairs."

Extremists that we are, we even reject the 10% discount offered by restaurants to "seniors." "But why?" ask the startled cashiers as they struggle to readjust the bill. Depending upon the sassiness of our mood, we answer thusly: "We're happy we can pay our own way, like *you* do;" or "It's good for our morale."

So, after resigning from our respective careers as a teacher and an engineer, and anticipating no graduations, weddings, or new grandchildren in the predictable future, we applied and were accepted for mission service in the West Indies.

As short-term missionaries, we enjoyed wonderfully challenging experiences. During the first year, Jim helped operate the Calvary Evangelistic Mission radio station in San Juan, Puerto Rico, and I assisted new mothers with postnatal care. During the second year, we managed WIVV, the Mission's radio station on the Caribbean island of Vieques, and we were on hand to help pick up the pieces after Hurricane Hugo smashed our tiny strip of land broadside.

Now the exciting two years were behind us and, winging northward in a crowded DC10, we felt suspended in space between two worlds. Suspended in time, also, along with thousands of our contemporaries, hovering tentatively somewhere between our "productive years" and the "end of the line."

"What are we going to do now?" I asked my hubby, engrossed in airline literature.

"Get off the plane," he answered patiently. "After it lands."

"Don't be clever. I mean what are we going to do with our lives? What do other people do—I mean the people like us?"

"Why don't you ask them?" Husbands are so practical.

"O. K. smarty, I will. And then—I'll write a book."

Jim sprang to attention and with his trusty camera lodged securely between his feet, he solemnly announced, "I'll be the photographer!"

"It's a deal!"

We shook on it and then, even as one, we leaned across the aisle and confided to a dozing stranger, *"We're* going to write a *book!"* (We learned long ago that you're much more likely to keep a commitment once you've heard yourself say it out loud to someone. *Any* one! It has the same dedicating effect as kneeling and facing east, or crossing your heart and hoping to die.)

Anyway, we made the commitment, and next came Plans and Procedures.

Observation has persuaded us that people who are of retirement age and are no longer employed at their career jobs fall loosely into three categories.

The Rockers are those people who retire only to sit and rock away their lives and do nothing except wait to die.

The Cruisers are those who spend most of their retirement time and money in pursuit of pleasure: a leisurely life style, travel, golf, fishing—all the things they couldn't do before.

The Part-timers are those who volunteer part of their retired lives to organized causes: literary programs; AIDS awareness; soup kitchens; food pantries; schools; libraries; building projects; homeless shelters; clothing exchanges; hospitals; nursing homes; environmental improvements; and on and on and on. (Let me say here that we have the highest regard and appreciation for volunteers. The world turns much more smoothly because of their efforts. Actually, up to this point, volunteerism was the only avenue we were aware of that offered post-career participation in society.

As we understood them, typical Part-timers volunteer part of one or two days a week toward the cause of their choice. The Cruisers cruise a couple months of the year. The Rock-ers rock year round.

Most retired folks, of course, fashion a mixture of these three lifestyles.

Surely, we reasoned, there must be a fourth group of self-propelled retired persons who, in addition to (or instead of) rocking, cruis-ing or part-time volunteering, have zeroed in on more time-consuming endeavors to build their lives around. These innovative individuals would have dug into the recesses of their minds, their forgotten dreams, their latent talents, their hobbies-on-hold, their unsatisfied ambitions. Through their own innovativeness, they would have attained a new focus for their existence, a reason to get up in the morning, a plan that enables them to face the rest of their lives with joy and anticipation.

This was the nebulous group, Group #4, the Self-starters, that piqued our curiosity and stirred our lazy imaginations. We wondered where were the people whose resourcefulness could inspire the rest of us to latch on to something interesting, exciting, remunerative, adventuresome, useful, daring, creative, fun, or none of the above, to fill the years that stretch ahead.

If they were out there somewhere, we would find them!

When the plane landed we would hug our many kids and grandkids hello and goodbye, hop into the car, and start driving.

We would not limit our search to a single community or a geographic region, but we would travel to each of the 50 states and personally discover men and women who typify the innovativeness and gumption we so admire. If a celebrity or two fell down in front of us, we wouldn't step around them. But our intent was to seek out plain, ordinary people, even as you and I, who had kicked over their rocking chairs and found unique, purposeful lives underneath.

Finally, we would share our discoveries with you. We would write 50 sketches about our newly acquired friends from 50 states and many walks of life who, though totally unknown to one another, are truly kindred spirits.

We undertook this adventure primarily for ourselves and our own mental and spiritual health, but it is also our hope that a reader or two will shake off his or her retirement lethargy and say, "Hey, I can avoid the retirement trap too!"

John King

"Noble be man, helpful and good."

Don Quixote, Cervantes

ALABAMA

John King

If you had walked a city route for years on end as a mail carrier, what's the first thing you would do after you retired?

That's exactly what John King did: sat down and rested.

But John is wiser than the run of the mill of us, and he soon realized that the sitting position is a hazardous one.

"I'm sorta on the lazy side," he confesses, "and if I hadn't found something to do right away, I'd probably be dead from inactivity by now."

John's idea for "something to do" had actually sprouted years before as he delivered letters up and down the familiar streets of Montgomery, Alabama. Day after day it had grieved him to see weeds thriving where there should have been flowers and vegetables. Big back yards stood neglected, producing nothing.

When the Montgomery Clean City campaign made wasteland available for garden plots a decade ago, John was a ringleader in the project.

Now John had more time. Now he could promote the art of agriculture in a personal way. He would help his neighbors become skilled gardeners. He would do it through persuasion, advice, and example.

But first John would need to increase the knowledge he had already gained from experience. He applied for help from the Agricultural Extension Service of the University of Alabama and eventually became certified as a master gardener. He continues to read avidly and takes full advantage of botanical information offered by state universities. This he shares freely with the community, and the results are obvious in the flourishing gardens of his neighborhood.

John has a garden too, but his current specialty is a beautiful arbor of muscatine grapes, which produce 50 gallons of wine a season.

The grapes he also shares with his neighbors — provided they do the picking.

The wine he hospitably shared with us — provided we critique the taste.

One sip. Two sips. Three . . . . What an exciting assignment for a couple of tee-totalers who were hitherto only qualified to compare the taste of Coca Cola to that of Pepsi!

Don Robinson

"The sky's the limit."

The Divine, Goethe

ALASKA

Don Robinson

Somehow we had not mentally prepared ourselves for Alaska, so we found it overwhelming: the mud flats, glaciers, Mt. McKinley, icebergs, wild animals, modern cities, remote wildernesses, avalanches, bush pilots and *airplanes* — 9,408 of them to be exact.

It was all those planes and the significance they play in the life of Alaska that led us to our Alaska subject, Don Robinson.

In a state with limited highways and railroads, airplanes are the chief means of transportation for business, pleasure and rescue work; and bush pilots were, and still are, an integral part of developing Alaska.

To dramatize that fact and to preserve the aviation history of Alaska, the Alaskan Heritage Museum sits smack dab in the middle of the Lake Hood floatplane base in Anchorage. That's where we discovered Don Robinson. Don was in the hangar, working away on a 1928 Stearman biplane, restoring it for a place of honor in the museum.

Don had repaired planes while he was in military service during World War II and the Vietnam war. There followed a long, predictable career in production with the Cyntex Pharmaceutical Company in Boulder, Colorado. When Don retired, however, he once again felt the enticing lure of the airways.

This time he planned to be in the pilot's seat.

Don could have stayed in Colorado and accomplished his goal, but the route to the air is less complicated and more accessible in Alaska. Besides, he had a couple of sons in Alaska, the scenery is great, and his wife, Thelma, had been offered a job as a pediatric nurse practitioner, traveling (by plane, no less) to far flung areas of the icebound state.

Don's first step toward his goal of piloting was to enroll at the Anchorage Community School of the University of Alaska and earn an aircraft and power plant license. This qualified him to work on everything from a 747 to a two-passenger Super Cub like the one he now co-owns with one of his sons.

The next step was to learn to fly, and that achievement is within sight—right down the runway of his life. In the meantime, Don obviously has become an expert in plane restoration and is equally adept at creating a missing part, painstakingly restoring an engine, or replacing portions of a fuselage. But Don does more than putter at the aviation museum, where he volunteers four days a week. He also offers visitors low-key lectures on the history and fate of the wrecked planes he renovates and the venturesome pilots who once navigated them.

No ordinary retirement existence for the extraordinary Don Robinson. He wanted to do something different with his life, and he has.

It isn't for everyone to retire and become a bush pilot on America's last frontier but, as Don says in his unassuming manner, "To each his own."

Eleanor Everhart

"Would you like to swing on a star, carry
moonbeams home in a jar?"

Swinging On A Star,
Johnny Burke & James Van Heusen

ARIZONA

Eleanor Everhart

Broadway Proper is a plush retirement condominium complex in Tucson, Arizona, which can hold its own with the best accomodations offered by Conrad Hilton. Six inch bouncy carpeting. Sparkling free-form pool. Elegant dining. Ample opportunities for effortless recreation. All the features designed to help well-to-do retirees exist in relaxation and ease. Eleanor Everhart lives at Broadway Proper because she chooses to and can afford to. But Ellie of the bright brown eyes is not your average affluent resident, although she is quick to admit she thoroughly revels in the luxurious setting. She especially enjoys her two daily laps around the aforementioned sparkling free-form pool.

Most of the time, however, Ellie is off and running, expanding her knowledge, trying her hand at all of the things she wanted to know and do but didn't have time for during her career as a department store merchandiser.

Ellie bought her condominium after her husband, William, died of cancer, and since then it has served as headquarters for "doing as much as I can do." "My husband wouldn't be proud of me if I didn't," she says wistfully.

Doing as much as she can do involves satisfying a super-avid curiosity and parlaying the results into action.

Useful action. Inspiring action. Goal oriented action.

For example, her curiosity about acting techniques inspired her to take classes at the Tucson Golden Age of Acting studio. The information she gained there thrust her toward teaching acting classes to her fellow residents in the condominium. On a regular basis, she directs them in original improvisational plays based upon their personal experiences. She also auditions regularly for movies being filmed on location when the script calls for an attractive, mature woman with short gray hair.

Ellie's innate curiousity for facts led her to help produce documentaries on such varied subjects as rodeos, the Valley of the Moon, AIDS, the return of the Tucson trolley, and the Mrs. Senior America national contest (in which Ellie was a finalist in her state).

Involvement in producing documentaries spawned Ellie's desire to learn more about the role of the person *behind* the camera. Without hesitation she applied to a television training program and in due time was proficient as a camcorder operator, studio technician, editor and control room operator. Certification in these skills qualified her to produce documentaries on her own, and she undoubtedly will.

Somewhere along the way Eleanor Everhart became curious about how it would feel to sky dive. She satisfied that curiosity by parachuting 9500 feet on her 70th birthday. (Ellie's medical records mention a heart prolapse and a broken leg, but these two items in no way relate to the parachute experience.)

She plans to sky dive again. We heard her say the words.

Johnie Howard

"You tell me your dream,
and I'll tell you mine."

You Tell Me Your Dream,
C. N. Daniels

ARKANSAS

Johnie Howard

Johnie Howard is a happy man, and why shouldn't he be? After all he's "the boss" now, and that's a title he's looked forward to holding since he was a little boy helping in his father's sawmill.

In his youth, Johnie hadn't minded carrying lumber and picking up wood scraps, but he always dreamed of being the man who sawed the wood; "the sawyer"; the boss, like his father. He dreamed of owning a sawmill himself some day.

Today, after a long career as an aviation electrician with the Air Force, Johnie is living out his dream, the dream that lingered persistently during his years in the service. When he retired, he followed the tug of his heart and, with his wife, Connie, and four children, went back to Arkansas, the familiar state of his youth. There, on a plot of inherited land, he set up his very own sawmill. And there we found him at dusk on a summer evening, nervously swatting mosquitos as he put his equipment to bed for the night.

It doesn't take many prerequisites to establish a sawmill, but Johnie Howard has them all: muscles; a strong desire; three pieces of well-worn equipment (a saw, a planer, and a power engine); two makeshift sheds; and a flat abandoned railroad bed on a high cliff overlooking a river.

Johnie uses the river to float huge logs from his acreage a few miles upstream. This involves the strenuous labor of felling the trees, rolling them to the water, tying them together in threes, and pulling them by boat, thirty at a time, down the river to the mill location.

There he meticulously saws them into boards suitable for decking, siding or fencing—the lumber most often requested by his customers.

Concerning customers, Johnie's attitude is refreshingly casual. If they spot his equipment and stop in, fine. If they pass on by, no matter. From word-of-mouth advertising, Johnie earns enough to supplement his retirement check and his wife's teaching salary.

Making money wasn't part of Johnie Howard's dream anyway. "I couldn't just do nothing, could I? I had to do something. And I always wanted to be a sawyer—like my dad."

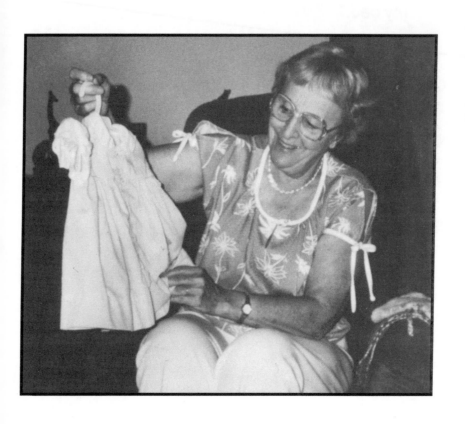

Maggie May

"Inasmuch as you have done it unto
one of the least of these . . ."

Matthew 25:40 (King James Version)

CALIFORNIA

Maggie May

Some people are addicted to cigarettes; some to alcohol; some to drugs; some to gambling; some to television.

Maggie May is addicted to garage sales. She can't exist without them. They're her driving force! In other words, she's hooked.

To satisfy her habit, Maggie avidly scans the classified ads of the local newspaper for garage sale locations. Experience has taught her that the early bird catches the bargains, and Maggie is a bargain hunter with the best of them.

So, while her less motivated friends are sipping their second cups of coffee, Maggie is lacing on her walking shoes or mounting her bike to depart on her never-ending quest for someone else's discards.

Her route takes her up and down the streets of Orange, California, covering the radius of a mile encircling the home she shares with her husband, Homer.

Fortunately, Homer is not the stereo-typical husband who grumbles at his wife's garage sale obsession. Rather, he is her chief supporter and cheerleader, because he realizes that tracking down bargains gives Maggie's days a purpose: to make the world a little bit brighter for the unfortu-nate—orphans, neglected children, babies of the homeless.

When Maggie retired as a school nurse some years ago ("They'd seen enough of me and I had seen enough of them"), she had no plan for the future, but she decided to get one. "Sit around? Not me!"

It was important to Maggie that her plan coincide with her strong urge to serve others in a unique and personal way. Ga-rage sales became the unexpected answer.

The "finds" which catch Maggie's eye are almost always children's clothing in good condition. When she gets home she spreads the day's purchases out on the floor for Homer to admire. Then she washes each little garment carefully, repairs snags or rips, and replaces missing but-tons.

Later, the clothing is lovingly delivered to orphans' homes, shelters for battered women and children, and homeless families.

Bargain hunting at garage sales an insignificant preoccupation? Maggie May would scoff at the idea. She would assure you it's her mission in life.

Ray Price

"...lest we forget..."
Recessional, Rudyard Kipling

COLORADO

Ray Price

"When you're going through life, you don't always have time to do everything you want to do."

We wondered and soon learned what caused the regret in the voice of the big, ruddy man who sat before us in his small apartment.

In his younger days, Ray Price had been a cowboy and later managed a million and a half acre cattle ranch in his native Colorado. With his experience in ranching, he had moved easily into jobs with governmental agencies that dealt with soil conservation, forestry and land control.

He had enjoyed it all, but his one consuming passion, the persistent interest he had never had time to pursue, was historical research.

In his retirement, there was time. To satisfy his curiosity and also to gather information to leave as a legacy to his children, Ray began delving into the genealogy of his own family. He soon discovered the exciting fact that his personal roots intertwined with those of Lilburn Wyecliff Boggs, an early governor of Missouri; Col. Sterling Price, also a Missouri governor; Kit Carson, the pioneer explorer; and Daniel Boone.

Now there was no stopping Ray Price, because all of these distant kinsmen had played integral roles in developing the rich traditions of the Colorado area of his birth.

Ray's search for his lineage not only expanded into a personalized account of Colorado history but also into a hands-on restoration of endangered landmarks.

The old "Governor Boggs home place" in Boggsville, Missouri, for example, had been crumbling before Ray organized and lead an effort to preserve it. He then turned his attention toward revising faded maps to verify original locations of Indian trading posts and an old Spanish fort on the Taos trail.

Ray also determined to recapture for posterity some of the ancient customs of the La Vita, Colorado, region. When we met him he was in the throes of making adobe bricks of clay, straw and a "secret" ingredient. Later, he would direct a crew of volunteers in building three *"hornos,"* authentic duplicates of large outside ovens used by the early Spanish settlers. A community feast featuring roast beef, bread, potatoes, corn on the cob, and fruit cobblers—all cooked in the new-old *hornos*—would celebrate the completion of the exciting project.

Ray Price's dream of helping to keep history alive is being fulfilled, but he laments the fact that more of his contemporaries are not writing down their memories for future generations to treasure. "If they could just share the knowledge they have, it would be so valuable. When they're gone, the knowledge will be gone, too . . . and that's sad."

Curtis Ambler

"Nobody is gonna rain on my parade."

Don't Rain On My Parade,
Bob Merrill & Jule Styne

CONNECTICUT

Curtis Ambler

"You don't have to be crazy (to spend at least 20 hours a week refurbishing old fire engines), but it helps," says Curtis Ambler with a characteristic twinkle in his eyes.

Curtis, along with a few like-minded buddies, has been enjoying his self-assigned occupation since he retired as a vice president of engineering for Stanley Tools.

In addition to pursuing his career profession, Curt had served as a volunteer fireman for 34 years in his hometown of Newington, Connecticut. During those years, he had seen many fire engines replaced by newer equipment and he decided to rescue at least a few of them for posterity in his retirement. Why let a bit of history slip into oblivion when he had the mechanical ability and love of antiques to preserve it for future generations?

Now housed in a large garage built by Curt and his fellow enthusiasts, sparkling, restored engines stand in readiness to parade down the streets of Newington behind the decorated floats, the Boy Scout troops and the high school band. Curt and his group are also continually on the alert to acquire and refurbish antique engines from other localities to add to their historical collection.

As is typical of many active retirees, Curtis Ambler's interests are not confined to a single area. Along with numerous participants in International Executive Service Corps, he has shared his expertise with struggling businesses in a third world country. In his spare moments he volunteers at the local children's hospital, serves as a city commissioner, and—in a perhaps more humble capacity—he keeps the heating system operating efficiently in his church.

"What would you tell other retired persons to help them enjoy life as much as you do?" I asked Curt Ambler.

"Nothing," was his terse reply. "If they're not self-motivated they won't listen anyhow."

With that, our self-motivated engineer, fireman, community servant, church caretaker and Renovator of Antique Fire

Engines posed jauntily behind the wheel of his latest restoration and added, "Too many retired people just dry up on the vine."

But not Curt Ambler. He'll be the one piloting the bright red antique fire engine in Newington's next parade. And you can be sure the sirens will be wailing!

Naomi Winchester

"Pass it on."

Pass It On, Kurt Kaiser

DELAWARE

Naomi Winchester

Here is a lady who not only dealt with the situation of retirement for herself, but decided to do something about it for other people.

Naomi Winchester had raised two daughters and enjoyed a long, exciting and satisfying career working with the Girl Scouts of America.

As retirement time approached, however, Naomi became increasingly aware of the older segment of the population—the segment she was beginning to identify with—that has needs equally as urgent as those of young people.

Naomi had worked out her own philosophy for the future: when you leave one job, go get another one! But what about the people who can no longer work? The unmotivated ones? The ones with poor health? The ones burdened with grief?

Helping those people find a full life—emotionally, physically, and spiritually—became Naomi's mission, but she realized immediately that she needed to be better prepared for her self-delegated assignment.

So back to college (a 90 mile daily round trip) went the unstoppable Naomi Winchester. Next came seminary, a master's degree, and ordination as a diaconal minister in the Methodist Church.

Now she was ready for her new career as a consultant on aging.

"Older people need to be stimulated, to be involved in some kind of socialization," she told us as we visited in her bustling office.

To get them involved is Naomi's object in life, and her present job with her religious denomination is the perfect vehicle for achieving her goal. Drawing from churches and community organizations, she has equipped herself with an endless resource list of interest groups, projects crying for volunteers, and centers for developing new skills.

Naomi encourages everyone within hearing range to keep learning, changing, serving!

"But most important of all," she adds with wry humor, "you have to get yourself out of bed!"

Gary Hilton

"Live it with gusto!"

Where Lies the Land,
William Wordsworth

FLORIDA

Gary Hilton

We discovered Gary Hilton lounging on the back bench of his commercial pleasure boat, which was tied up at a touristy port in the Gulf of Mexico. He was tall, bronze, athletic and handsome, with a dazzling shock of white hair and an equally dazzling smile.

We knew instinctively that he was our "retiree" candidate for the state of Florida. No man could radiate such an aura of complete contentment as Gary Hilton and still be struggling to earn a living in a stressful job!

At the precise moment of our discovery, Gary was waiting for his group of boisterous passengers to emerge from a dockside pub. He would then transport them by water to a series of ports where they would disembark, continue partying, and re-embark throughout the evening.

Conducting party cruises is not Gary's only pursuit, however. He also operates what is familiarly known along vacation waterfronts as a "dive shop," not to be confused with a dive (as in sleazy saloon). Gary's shop is well stocked with sportswear and all the equipment necessary for fishing, snorkeling, or scuba diving. It also features one of the few fully certified diving instructors in Florida, namely Gary himself.

When he isn't teaching diving or running his store, Gary is happily piloting a boatload of vacationers on scuba diving, sightseeing, snorkeling, or fishing trips into the gulf, and reveling in every minute of it.

"Salt water is magnetic," he told us. "It draws me like nothing else does."

Gary and his wife, Francine, raised their family in a midwestern state. During those busy years, Gary resolutely resisted the lure of the water to concentrate on building a successful career as general agent of a large insurance company. Finally the day came when Gary made the inevitable pronouncement: "You only go around once. You may be living in a beautiful home and making lots of money, but if you're not doing what you really enjoy doing, then what's it all about anyway?"

Not much, was the answer. So Gary packed up his willing family, moved to Florida, and today is doing what he really enjoys. He is working enough to keep from feeling useless, relishing his freedom, and loving the feel of the wind at his back and the smell of salty water in his nose.

Ray and Shirley Pierce

"Yes, we have no bananas . . ."

Yes, We Have No Bananas,
Frank Silver & Irving Cohn

GEORGIA

Shirley and Ray Pierce

Need directions to find a winning attitude in the face of major disappointment? Here they are. Start from any point in the Chicago area some sunny, spring morning and drive south/southeast a thousand miles (more or less) until you bump into Savannah, Georgia. Get on Route 80 and keep going forever until you come to a big green bank. Turn left at the bank, and left again at the first street after you cross the railroad tracks. Turn right at the third block and start looking for the house with a yellow Pontiac in the driveway.

That's where you'll find Shirley and Ray Pierce, successfully mending their lives back together after circumstances dealt them a low blow: retirement status long before they expected it, wanted it, or were ready for it.

Actually, Shirley was not at home when we arrived after our long trip. It was one of the three days each week that she works for a hospice program, attending terminally ill patients in their homes.

The Pierces have seven adult children. While the kids were young, effervescent Shirley was a contented full time mother. When Ray unexpectedly and prematurely found himself at the end of a successful career as personnel director of several large hospitals, Shirley met the challenge. Off she went to become a Certified Nurse Assistant. First serving as a volunteer, she was soon offered a paying position and is now working outside the home for the first time in her life.

For big, genial Ray, the change in job status was not so easy. As he explains it, "The balloon popped."

Ray used the long, empty months that followed his unwelcome retirement struggling to "stay out of the pits," reexamining his values, and becoming acquainted with himself in a new role—that of a now unemployed administrator. He also painted up, cleaned up, and fixed up everything he could lay his hands on to keep busy.

"You gotta be doing something," Ray says convincingly, "or you'll go bananas." (Obviously Ray didn't "go bananas," and he posed beside a totally banana-less banana tree in their back yard to demonstrate the point.)

Without doubt the most dominant factor that influenced Ray's victory over discouragement was the opportunity he took to study for and become a permanent deacon in the Catholic Church. This position is so obviously meaningful to him that it flavors much of his conversation.

Eventually, Ray landed a three day a week job as a salesman of restaurant equipment, and he loves it. With determination, optimism, and a healthy sense of self worth, Ray and Shirley Pierce have transformed premature retirement into an ideal lifestyle: both of them are "out in the world" part of the week happily working and earning money, but they still have many days each week to spend together or to visit their children.

Need further directions to the Pierce's reconstruction project? Don't stop on the railroad tracks!

George Fujinaga

"Footprints in the sands of time."

A Psalm of Life,
Henry Wadsworth Longfellow

HAWAII

George Fujinaga

We had expected our once-in-a-lifetime flight to Hawaii to be exciting. And it was. We had expected to have *leis* hung around our necks when we landed. And they were. We had expected the air to smell like heady perfume. And it did.

At this point, however, our expectations hit a snag. We had expected Hawaii to abound with interesting retirees from the mainland, all of them capable of inspiring a chapter in our book. And it doesn't. Actually, to our surprise, retirees from the mainland are pretty scarce in Hawaii, due to the high cost of Island living.

Quick switch to Plan B.

Our retiree radar telepathy system promptly went into operation and in no time at all we found ourselves in the presence of George Fujinaga, a likely interview subject for sure.

George is a native Hawaiian who

demonstrated to us in short order that retirees on any latitude or longitude can live purposeful lives if that's what they have decided to do.

When George suffered a back injury that forced him to stop working as a laborer, he knew he had to find a project to pour his energy into. "With nothing to do, I'd waste my life away. People are supposed to keep moving or they'll die."

George's father was Japanese and his mother Polynesian—not an unusual combination in Hawaii. Pure Polynesians are becoming rare, however, and there is an urgent effort being made in the islands to preserve authentic symbols of Polynesian culture. George Fujinaga is dedicating his retirement years to furthering that movement in a very tangible and unique way.

George had always cherished a primitive implement known as a *"poi* pounder," which once hung in his mother's kitchen. *Poi* pounders are used to mash the cooked, starchy, potato-like root of the native taro plant. *Poi,* the pastey substance that results, is still a favorite food on the islands. Although modern day *poi* pounders are now being mass produced, the antique utensil belonging to the Fujinaga family is one of the few "originals" remaining in Hawaii.

George determined to reproduce his mother's *poi* pounder by hand from basalt stone—splitting, hammering, pulverizing, shaping and sanding it into a glassy-smooth form just as his ancestors had done. To assure himself that the arduous, near-extinct process will live on after him, he willingly devotes a full year to teaching young apprentices his hands-on craft.

With characteristic independence, George Fujinaga refuses to sell the *poi* pounders he has made. His steadily increasing collection stands on simple shelves in the living room of his home and will some day be divided among his three adult children.

As George explains it, money is no longer an object. He has worked hard all his life, and now, in his words, he's "just gliding in."

George Fujinaga's only desire is to leave behind a legacy of irreplaceable Polynesian culture to his family and to the Hawaii he loves.

Jack Woods

"Nothing succeeds like success."

Ange Pitou, Alexander Dumas

IDAHO

Jack Woods

If there is one word that separates the men from the boys, the winners from the losers in any age group, that word is "motivation." For my money, Jack Woods invented the word.

Jack's career job had been selling insurance. A member of the fourth generation of his family to represent Farmer's Insurance Company, Jack had motivated himself to become district manager in the Lewiston, Idaho, office. In that position, he had taken pride in motivating the salespersons under him to help build the Lewiston agency into a highly successful business.

Insurance was clearly Jack's love until one day he decided that enough was enough. Surely it was time to slow down, let up on the pressure, cut back on his payroll, and begin enjoying the fruits of his financial success.

"If you save it all till you're old," he reasoned briefly, "you may not have the mental or physical ability to enjoy it." Instead of slowing down, however, Jack decided to jump in on a sudden building boom in Lewiston. Just for fun, he experimented with directing his motivational skills toward carpenters instead of insurance salespersons, and he quickly discovered that in any occupation the same principles apply: Set a goal! Get started! Keep moving!

Jack Woods once dreamed the familiar dreams of the Rockers and the Cruisers, but he was determined that those dreams would never dominate his life. He and his wife, Leona, might add a room to their house, cruise in the Caribbean, follow the sun in their mobile home, and golf the year around. But always Jack will motivate himself toward a goal, and never, never, never will he "think old," because, as he says, "If you start thinking old, you're going to *be* old."

Jack's most recent objective for self-motivation fell into his lap unexpectedly. (That all retirees should be so lucky!) An acquaintance had invented a simple device for identifying plants in a garden, and he offered to sell the potential business to Jack. Entrepreneur that he is, Jack bought the idea, samples, and equipment; set up an efficient shop in his back yard; and found himself in business once again.

Gone is his restlessness. Gone are some of their leisurely trips. Now Jack and Leona often use their mobile home to travel from state to state promoting a product which has caught on like wildfire. Their only problem: they have to put on the brakes occasionally to keep from earning too much money.

Enough said for motivation!

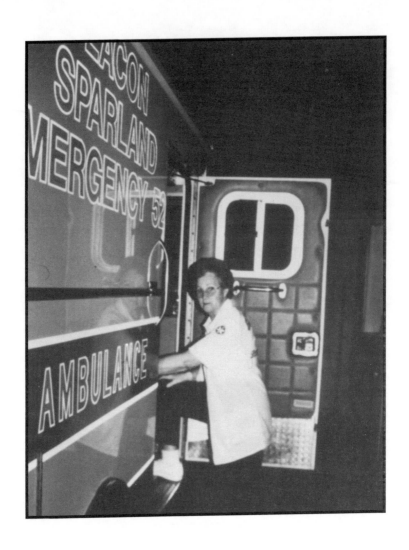

Margaret Gilbert

"A service beyond all recompense."

Surena, Pierre Corneille

ILLINOIS

Margaret Gilbert

Delivering a baby in an ambulance roaring full speed ahead with its sirens wide open is not the average woman's idea of retirement bliss.

But then, Margaret Gilbert of Lacon, Illinois, is not exactly average, although she insists that many other women could do what she does if they were willing to (1) be trained and (2) give the time. Even if they aren't up for heart attacks, auto wrecks, water accidents, buttons stuck in noses, and baby deliveries, they could opt for escort service at a hospital or assist in an emergency room.

Margaret goes the whole route as an Emergency Medical Technician, and she loves the excitement of ambulance duty—a far cry from the uneventful sales person routine she formerly followed.

The opportunity to "make people feel better where they're hurting" compensates for the inconvenience she experiences and the long period of preparation for her job she endured. The initial preparation included two nights a week for three and a half months to acquire the necessary 120 hours of training to become certified as an EMT, and that was only the beginning. Every two years, Margaret must reinforce her knowledge to be re-certified as a technician, and she updates her CPR techniques yearly.

In a rural area 30 miles from the nearest hospital, the 3500 scattered residents surrounding Lacon are entirely dependent upon their local ambulance in emergencies. The fully equipped vehicle was financed by donations, and the ambulance crew works strictly on a volunteer basis. But as Margaret says, "If I were doing it for money, it wouldn't be nearly so rewarding."

Margaret's husband, Leon, a former machinist, also serves the community by repairing ambulance parts in his back yard machine shop.

Leon has no idea how much longer his wife will continue to schedule their lives around a beeper signal. He only knows that recently Margaret felt duty bound to remind her much younger co-workers on the ambulance crew: "I'm a great-grandmother. Re-

member? I just celebrated another birthday. What do you want me to do about
quitting?"

"Shut up and sit down," was their
blunt but affectionate answer.

Margaret shut up.

And sat down.

In the ambulance.

Pauline and Paul Heffley

"To labor and not ask for any reward."

Prayer for Generosity,
Saint Ignatius Loyola

INDIANA

Pauline and Paul Heffley

Hurrying out of a crisp October evening into the warmth of their cozy living room was like stepping into a dream: the perfect setting where any couple could happily spend their retirement years in comfort and leisure, surrounded by friends and familiar possessions.

Even the smell of a pot roast cooking in the kitchen was part of the dream. Add to that family pictures; treasured art work from children and grandchildren; an old pump organ; mementos from distant lands where Paul had served in the U. S. Air Force; hand made crafts; a huge stone fireplace; and, visible through glass doors, a long porch overlooking a creek winding through their very own woods.

"I guess you guys realize you have it made," I said to Pauline and Paul Heffley. "I don't see how anyone could ever leave this house."

"Oh, we leave it all the time," was their breezy answer. "In fact, we're getting ready to go away again right now—but we wouldn't go anywhere if we didn't think there was a need."

We soon learned about the "need" that compels this husband and wife to up-root themselves on a regular basis and lock the doors of their dream house behind them. They definitely feel "called" to the West indies to work with Calvary Evangelistic Mission, which operates two Christian radio stations in Puerto Rico.

Paul and Pauline provide their own travel and living expenses while on the islands, doing anything and everything within their capabilities to be helpful. Here are two people, neither of whom has a highly developed skill to contribute, but both of whom have a willingness to fit in wherever they can: painting, sewing, repairing, gardening, grading Bible correspondence lessons, even "working the board" (which is broadcast jargon for pressing buttons and pulling switches to make programs play out from a radio station).

It's probably no coincidence that the wall hanging which captured our attention in the Heffley's Indiana home reads, "Lives are full of happiness when hearts are full of love."

Wes Jespersen

"Small service is true service."
To a Child, William Wordsworth

IOWA

Wes Jespersen

"An humble and handsome man." "One in a million." "A highly respected citizen." "Mr. Cleanup." "Council Bluff's bicycle riding ecologist."

These are some of the phrases we had heard describing Wes Jespersen before we knocked on the door of his small, third floor apartment. We also had been informed that Wes was retired, in poor health, and lived alone. How did these vital statistics mesh with the accolades listed above?

We soon found out. It is in the role of self-appointed environmentalist that Wes Jespersen has gained the respect and admiration of Council Bluffs, Iowa.

Except for a few part time painting jobs, Wes's wage-earning career ended when the apartment building he maintained was destroyed by fire. Since then, although unwell, Wes has concentrated his efforts on

making America—specifically his city—
more beautiful.

Equipped solely with a bicycle, Wes, on his own initiative and on a regular basis, wheels the length and breadth of Council Bluffs, picking up cans and trash and stuffing it into plastic bags to be hauled away later by city trucks. On one day alone he filled 45 bags, but that meant working from sunrise to sunset. "Riding my bike and picking up garbage is good therapy," he explains cheerfully. "It's hard work, but I love it. If you enjoy what you're doing, that's half the battle."

For his effort, Wes is repaid only in appreciation, and that's just the way he wants it. His constant desire is that more of his fellow citizens would catch the idea and start bending down and picking up.

Wes finds the state of the world more than a little discouraging. With characteristic sense of responsibility, he muses that the obvious solution is for each of us "to give joy and happiness and love to make things better for everyone."

On his days off, Wes helps out at the community food pantry or mingles with the other apartment building dwellers. He deliberately limits his mingling activities, however, because "most of the residents just sit around all day twiddling their thumbs and talking about their neighbors."

Thumb twiddling is definitely not Wes Jespersen's dish. "I'm planning on picking up trash as long as my back holds out," he says.

Then what?

"Well, I guess I'll get a brace and keep going.'"

Helen and Ken Simons

"It is only a moment here and a moment there
that the greatest writer has."

Collected Poems, Robert Frost

KANSAS

Ken Simons

Ken and Helen Simons were cordial as they met us at the door of their well kept, sunny ranch home in Pittsburg, Kansas. They were up for being interviewed, but they politely conveyed the message that our time with them was limited. Clearly, we had been sandwiched between an appointment down town and a short cat nap.

After all, Ken is 87 and Helen sees to it that he gets his rest—but not too much of it. "If you lie down in bed you might not get up," explains Ken. "That's why I don't go to bed any more than I have to."

Ken Simons knows what busy schedules and meeting deadlines are all about. For most of his long career he served as managing editor of the *Morning Sun*, Pittsburg's flourishing newspaper. Later he was a four-time award winning columnist, and he has framed certificates on the crowded walls of his tiny home office to prove it.

When Ken stopped going to the newspaper plant on a daily basis, he continued to submit a bi-weekly column to the paper.

"But why didn't you quit," I asked, fully anticipating his answer. "I'd have died, that's the reason. I had to keep my mind active."

Ken presently writes his column twice a week, and that's enough to keep his mind active according to plan. He reads a lot, gathers information by phone, meets with his cronies in one of the town's coffee shops, and dips into his storehouse of recollections for subject material.

The written pieces that result are varied and clever, and they often jab the slumbering memories of his readers.

One of his columns explored the length of time it takes a man to shave. Another offered first hand, bittersweet advice on what to expect when you attend your 50th college reunion. Still another colorfully described the blow by blow account of his own birth (although this report was admittedly based upon hearsay).

At this point in our visit, we realized that we had been courteously but firmly propelled to the doorway and were being told a pleasant goodbye by our smiling host and hostess.

Far be it from us to upset the schedule of a busy 87 year old writer with a destination!

Nona Smoot

"A truer friend there cannot be than
one who shares her recipe."

Author unknown

KENTUCKY

Nona Smoot

We had to wait several hours for Nona Smoot to finish cleaning a doctor's office in the small town of Williamsburg, Kentucky. We spent the time thinking about Nona as she had already been described to us by the townspeople.

A woman of dignity, friendly and dependable, who had worked off and on for years in local restaurants, sometimes cleaning offices to supplement her income or just "help out;" a widow who had nursed her husband, Nobel, through a long terminal illness; an excellent cook who, by popular demand, was now establishing a catering business out of her own kitchen.

Catering was an easy transition from restaurant cooking, as we learned from Nona later, when she bustled in from her cleaning job.

"I didn't need much advertising," she admits. "One friend told another, and that friend told another . . ." and pretty soon

Nona had her hands full cooking for receptions, showers, weddings, picnics and dinners. Once in a while it's necessary to call on a daughter or a sister to help. But most of the time Nona operates alone at breakneck speed. "When I get working I don't like to fool around with anyone who can't move as fast as I do."

My stomach began sending me messages as Nona talked about the menus she helps plan: the steamed vegetable tray with hot butter sauce, the Kentucky old ham and biscuits, her original cheese balls. But when she described her very special lemon pound cake, not to be found in any recipe book, I feverishly whipped out my pencil. Here is her recipe, word for word:

"You cream together 1/2 C. margarine, 1/2 C. Crisco, 4 eggs, 2 C. sugar, 1 1/2 t. salt, 1/2 t. soda, 1/2 t. baking powder, 1 C. buttermilk, 1 T. lemon juice. Then you add 3 C. flour (no, no, not self rising) and bake at 350 degrees for one hour in a 9 x 12 cake pan. While the cake is baking, mix together 1/2 pound of confectioners sugar, 3 T. orange juice, 2 T. lemon juice and 1/2 t. salt. When the cake is done, punch holes in the top with a fork and pour this second mixture over it. Pop the cake back in the oven for three minutes, and that's all there is to it. This cake freezes well and gets better and better all the time."

You can take it from us. We took it from Nona Smoot!

Sam Peters

"You can't take it with you."

You Can't Take It With You,
Moss Hart & George Kaufman

LOUISIANA

Sam Peters

Have you ever wondered what a "re-tired" man does with his money when he has more than he really needs? We happily found a man in Louisiana who demonstrates the answer: He DOES with his money!

Sam Peters doesn't fit your basic rich-man-born-with-a-silver-spoon-in-his-mouth syndrome, inasmuch as he came from a relatively modest background. At an early age, he was indoctrinated by his parents with a healthy respect for work, and along with that indoctrination came many homey adages which still pepper his conversation and influence his philosophy. ("Everyone is an expert in something. Discover your ability and use it!")

It so happens that Sam's ability is in the field of finance. After saxophoning his way through college, he became a certified public accountant and was offered a consulting job with a gigantic international company. After 49 years of ever-increasing responsibility and prestige with the same company, Sam did not retire; he simply changed directions.

Now the focus of Sam's life is not on how to make money but how to use it— and himself—for the greatest good. For him, the greatest good means giving back to his community some of the advantages and happiness which his community has given him throughout the years.

His gift of appreciation is expressed not merely in wealth, however, but also in effort. Sam has an extraordinary talent for fund-raising ("Plan your work and work your plan"), and he tirelessly enlists his fellow citizens in worthy pursuits. Some of the beneficiaries of his "push-prod-challenge-exemplify" fund-raising endeavors are his alma mater, Centenary Methodist College ("The only solution to the ills of the world is education based on Judeo-Christian ethics of morality"); community churches; his city's improving symphony orchestra; and many individuals and civic projects.

"But not every retired person has the position or the clout—or the money—to make the kind of contributions you're able to make," I ventured to suggest. This he acknowledged unabashedly but added that everyone has *something* to offer. ("Delineate your interest. Do the things that appeal. Get out in the public. Volunteer.")

Easy enough for a retired millionaire to say, I thought, while he basks on his yacht or shuttles between his three beautiful homes. My cynical thought was short-lived however, when I realized that this friendly retired millionaire also devotes more than half of his time working for the causes in which he has invested his money. And he does it joyously, modestly, and energetically because, after all, he insists with a final familiar platitude, "It is better to wear out than to rust out!"

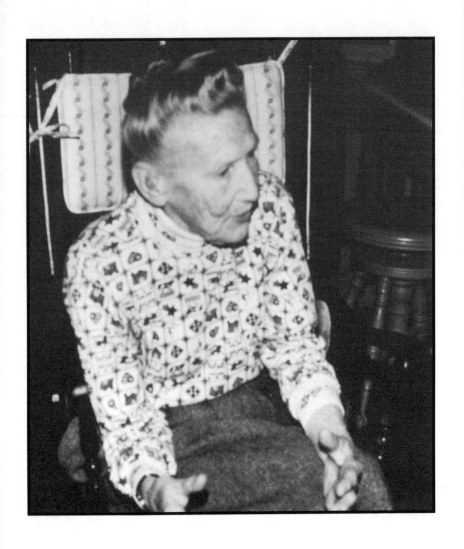

Carolyn Blouin

"It is better to light just one little candle
than to stumble in the dark."

One Little Candle,
George Mysels & J. Maloy Roach

MAINE

Carolyn Blouin

She had been described as a "feisty lady who works for causes." Since feisty ladies have a special appeal for us, we wasted no time in locating the 200-year-old Maine farm house where Carolyn Blouin lives with her husband, Maurice.

We did a poorly concealed double take when Carolyn herself opened the door and totally shattered our mental picture of the burly, aggressive, banner-waving woman we thought we had come to interview.

Carolyn Blouin is tiny, gracious, fragile. And she is 83 years old. Not your typical female activist.

Noting our state of shock, Carolyn put us at ease by recalling a similar incident. Once, as part of a large crowd of protesters, she overheard a much younger fellow marcher exclaim, "Look at that old woman! What the hell is she doing here?"

Undeterred, Carolyn continued to march. And she marches to this day, making her beliefs known by carrying placards, attending meetings, organizing telephone campaigns, writing letters, getting out the vote.

Carolyn acquired her first taste of crusading during the Civil Rights movement of the 1960's, and she was influential in gaining permission for a black student to apply for admission to a prestigious southern college.

She was in the Washington throng that heard Martin Luther King, Jr., give his "I have a dream" speech, and the memory of that experience has never faded. Even today, King's words inspire her to be concerned about the issues she considers to be vitally important: crime, health care, abortion, protection of the environment, use of the land, recycling, disintegration of family life, influence of the media, euthanasia, education, and the deplorable condition of partisan politics—and those are just for starters!

"There's so much to be excited about!" Carolyn Blouin says convincingly.

I found myself marveling that an 83 year old woman could still be up for excitement, when most people her age are content to sit back and watch the world go by. Carolyn must have read my mind and volunteered, "I don't complain and I don't worry. Worry gets in the way of doing other things, and there are so many *other* things that need to be done to save the world. Everyone can do something."

But what, I wondered.

"You have to look inside yourself and decide what you can do. It doesn't have to be big. It just has to be what *you* can do."

And then you have to do it!

Albert L. Young, Sr.

"He that is greatest among you
shall be your servant."

Matthew 23:11 (King James Version)

MARYLAND

Albert L. Young, Sr.

We discovered Deacon Albert L. Young, Sr., in Guilford, Maryland, polishing the front glass entrance of the small church he serves. He swung open the church doors and welcomed us with a broad smile and outstretched arms, and we soon realized that those outstretched arms typify Albert's total philosophy toward life in general. Reach out!

Long before he retired as a driver and maintenance man for the Federal Communications Commission, Albert had been reaching out to his community. After he collected his last pay check from the FCC, he didn't waste much time wondering how he would fill his extra hours. He already knew. To him extra hours only meant extra opportunities to help others.

Albert assessed his abilities and possessions to determine how best he could make himself useful, and he quickly recognized that his special vehicle for service was parked right in his own driveway. Who would expect a small battered pickup truck to provide the means for building a happy, rewarding retirement occupation? But that's exactly what happened.

For 24 hours a day, Albert and his truck make themselves available—totally free of charge—to fill a need, whatever the need might be. Sometimes they carry a sick or elderly person to the store or to a doctor; sometimes they rescue the household possessions of an evicted family and transport them to an empty warehouse for temporary storage; sometimes they collect newspapers for recycling; sometimes they deliver donated clothing and used furniture to residents who are down on their luck.

"I didn't want to put my feet up," says Albert L. Young, Sr.

Albert's wife, Shirley, hopes her husband never changes his mind. She knows that Albert, with his feet up, would be unhappy indeed.

And so would the community he serves.

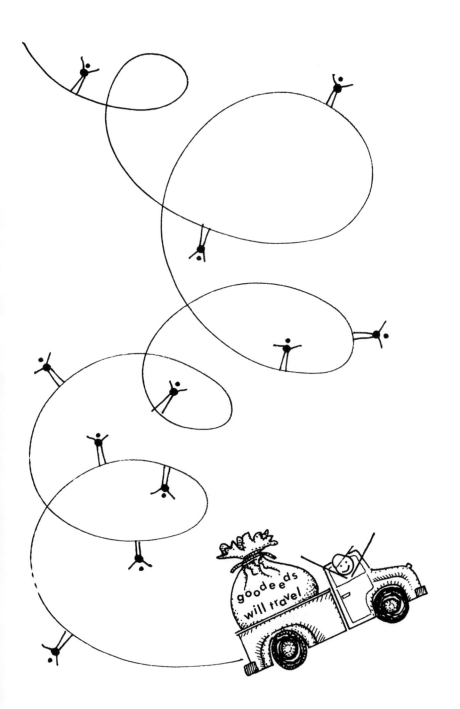

Ernie Knowlton

"He knows not his own strength
that hath not met adversity"

Moral Essays, Seneca

MASSACHUSETTS

Ernie Knowlton

We had approached the neat Massachusetts home of Ernie and Viola Knowlton with trepidation. How do you talk to a man about a fulfilling retirement when that man is a victim of advanced lung cancer? After all, hadn't we almost come to believe that "fulfilling retirement" is synonymous with "good health"?

Not so. Our first five minutes with the Knowltons totally disproved that idea.

Ernie, with his optimistic wife, Viola, at his side, had just completed 15 days of out-patient radiology treatments. One arm was in a sling and all of his movements were torturously slow and painful.

By his personal description of himself, Ernie is an independent, proud, Yankee man. By observation, he is a courageous, independent, proud, Yankee man who loves his wife, his family, his church, his lodge, music, beauty, travel and *work*.

Until emphysema took over, Ernie's work had been as managing engineer of plant facilities of a large Greenfield, Massachusetts, factory and, in his own words, his work kept him "as happy as a pig in mud." Then came cancer and forced retirement. But if he couldn't continue to do the job he enjoyed, reasoned Ernie, then he would learn to do something different and enjoy that! Remembering a famous comedian's advice to "shoot at the moon and you won't shoot your foot," Ernie began studying and experimenting with a new occupation, carving wood. Conveniently, he discovered the raw material for his project in the cedar, pine, mahogany and peach trees growing in his yard.

His "shot at the moon" has afforded him hundreds of hours of productive effort that have resulted in many intricate and strikingly beautiful pieces of wood art.

Ernie keeps up with his music, also. Even though he can no longer play in a band as he once did for diversion, he still can prop his bad arm on the keyboard and accompany group singing at church and at monthly lodge meetings.

"The more you do, the more you *can* do," is Ernie Knowlton's motto. As we left his home, another long forgotten line from the author, Hugh Walpole, surfaced in our memory: "It isn't life that matters. It's the courage you put into it."

June Elizabeth Robinson

"All experience is an arch, to build upon."

The Education of Henry Adams,
Henry Brooks Adams

MICHIGAN

June Elizabeth Robinson

"It's a lovely time to live!"

We had bumped, bounced and jolted down endless back roads of Michigan to locate June Elizabeth Robinson, the author of that line. And there was more: "All the things you have tucked away in your heart and your mind—now is the time to open the floodgates and let them all come out!"

"Opening the floodgates" is exactly what June is doing. And some of the things tucked away in her heart and mind include living through World War II in England and being at various times a dairy maid, artist, engraver, nurse, recreational specialist for the Royal Canadian Air Force, physical training instructor, department store salesperson, YWCA worker with children, horse trainer, dog groomer, writer, production manager of a traveling drama group, and amateur actress. Take a deep breath, because she still seeks worlds to conquer!

It's easy to understand how this talented and enthusiastic lady with the varied background arrived at her unusual avocational pursuit: writing original scripts based on simple Bible stories and directing groups of children as they present Christian drama throughout the area.

June had often observed that little children—including her own grandkids—are woefully turned off by church sermons worded primarily for adult listeners. How to capture the kids' attention? How to eliminate the misbehavior that results from their boredom?

What better solution than to provide an opportunity for the children to participate in the church service in a con-structive, rather than de-structive way? What better way for them to participate than through drama? (Children love to act.) Who better to write and direct the dramas than herself? (June loves to write and direct.)

The questions and answers fell into place neatly. June went to work adapting biblical stories into plays. Recollections of many of the roles she filled in her early life help her build realistic characterizations. Sharing her experiences also cements strong relationships with her young protegés.

For their part, the children work on innovating scenery out of cardboard boxes and whatever else is at hand. Under their director, they are being introduced to drama with a purpose and are learning simple techniques of staging and acting.

As for June Elizabeth Robinson, life is far from over. In her words, everything that happened in her busier years was leading her toward "this lovely space" where she can do the things she couldn't do before.

Dick and Dorothy Humes

"You're as welcome as the
flowers in May."

Love á lá Mode, Charles Macklin

MINNESOTA

Dorothy and Dick Humes

If you've raised nine children who are now grown and gone, and you own a multi-bedroom home in a vacationer's paradise, then you're eligible to open a bed and breakfast inn.

Dorothy and Dick Humes of Duluth, Minnesota, considered the requirements and decided they were ready for the job.

In addition to having their children out of the house, a lot of space, and a prime location, the Humes had these qualifications: their nine bedroom home is a veritable mansion overflowing with views, priceless antiques, and fireplaces that work; Dorothy and Dick are in excellent health; Dorothy's supplementary income as a nurse banishes the Bed and Breakfast Beginning Business Blues; and, quite strategically, the couple has a grown daughter who lives nearby and fills in when the need arises.

Actually, the Humes insist that the "nearby daughter" is the most essential ingredient for their success. If you don't have one, then borrow one, they advise all prospective bed and breakfast inn operators, because the job is extremely confining and innkeepers are notoriously susceptible to burnout.

Notwithstanding, Dorothy and Dick revel in their retirement venture, and their joy in sharing their hospitality with their guests compensates for any inconvenience.

For Dick, becoming an innkeeper merely meant shifting gears from the career job he enjoyed as director of Duluth's Department of Housing and Rehabilitation. In that pursuit he helped provide permanent living accommodations for the elderly, the ill, and the underprivileged. As an innkeeper he now helps provide temporary living accommodations for vacationers, business persons, and honeymooners.

The success of the Humes' Barnham House Bed and Breakfast is undoubtedly due to the personal touch of its owners. Dick sometimes works 18 hours a day scheduling reservations, doing the book work, and maintaining the property in picture perfect condition. He confides that his energy is inspired by Dorothy, who keeps going . . . and going . . . and going . . . .

She is up at the crack of dawn, making a list and checking it twice to assure that the day ahead runs efficiently. Before she leaves for her nursing job, she whips up one of her tempting breakfast specialties for their visitors: homemade coffee cake, or hash browns, quiche or bacon popovers.

It's just one more little gesture of hospitality with which Dorothy and Dick Hume welcome their bed and breakfast guests—including two road-weary strangers armed with notebook and camera.

Hal and Dot Buchanan

"How beautiful . . . are the feet of those
who bring good tidings."

Isaiah 52:7 (King James Version)

MISSISSIPPI

Dot and Hal Buchanan

Dot and Hal Buchanan are a classic example of a couple who combined the training and experience of their former careers to produce a busy and rewarding retirement.

Hal had spent his adult life as a teacher, principal, and school superintendent. Dot had been a librarian. The obvious requisites for each of their jobs were advanced education, organizational ability, and a high regard for learning. In other words, BOOKS. Add to these attributes their mutual desire to serve those in need and it is understandable that the Buchanans are now a vital, volunteer two-person operation which collects, sorts, and ships Christian books in English to library-deprived countries all over the world.

Dot and Hal got the idea for their new career from International Book Project, an establishment which collects and dispenses miscellaneous reading material worldwide. The Buchanans promptly recognized a specific need for Christian resource books not supplied by that secular organization but desperately needed by missionaries, seminaries, pastors and students in under-developed nations.

Calling their project "Book Link," they began soliciting donations of used or new books, tapes and journals from churches, pastors, and individuals all over the United States. The books trickled in, and then poured in, and so did requests for them from Christian workers in five states and 45 countries around the world who had gradually received news of their service.

When we visited the Buchanans in the small office-storage room attached to their home, their Book Link project had been in operation about two years. In that period, some 30,000 resource items had been shipped by them on request, and Dot and Hal Buchanan eagerly await more of both: books *and* requests.

Judging by the pile of requests stacked on their desk and the supply of materials lining the walls, however, there appears to be no letup ahead for this tire-

less couple. If they should manage to
sneak a short vacation, more than likely
they would volunteer as short term missionaries and check out the book shelves in
Nigeria . . . or the Philippines . . . or
Uganda . . . or Zambia . . . or Liberia . . . .

Dudley Thompson

"Gladly will he learn, and gladly teach."

The House of Fame, Chaucer

MISSOURI

Dudley Thompson

A devastating personal tragedy re-shaped the routine, the attitude, and the philosophy of Dudley Thompson for his retirement years.

Dr. Thompson is the vice chancellor emeritus of the University of Missouri, Rolla Campus, the former dean of faculty, the former chairman of the department of chemical engineering, a retired army colonel, and a contributor to his community through numerous government, church and civic organizations. With that noteworthy background, Dr. Thompson rightfully could have anticipated a rewarding retirement life basking in the afterglow of his accomplishments.

If Dudley ever entertained such a pleasant dream of the future, that dream came to an abrupt halt when his wife, Effie, began showing symptoms of Alzheimer's disease.

This was more than 15 years ago,

long before the current avalanche of information on Alzheimer's was available. He
was as stunned and ignorant as any husband would have been at the traumatic turn
of events. He soon realized that, in spite of
his advanced college degrees, the degree
of love for his wife was the only degree that
had prepared him for the challenging years
ahead.

So, with the help of nurses and the
curiosity characteristic of a scholar, Dr.
Thompson determined to learn as much as
possible about the shattering Alzheimer's
disease. It now became the primary focus
of his retirement to gather medical facts
pertinent to his needs as the caretaker and
his wife's needs as the patient.

The accumulated information he
photocopied and organized into a massive
reference book, making it available to other
Alzheimer's victims and their families in his
community. In what must have been a
forerunner to the numerous and varied
support groups in vogue today, Dudley
began meeting monthly with fellow townspeople to enlighten and encourage those
who shared the common heartache of a
loved one with Alzheimer's disease.

Dudley Thompson has continued to practice and advocate the lessons he learned during his wife's illness and death: do everything in your power to overcome physical impairment; stay busy; try to discover a constructive approach to the negative events of life; learn new skills; teach; remain active *outside* yourself.

Despite his unique combination of academic education and native good judgement, Dudley Thompson resorts to a commonplace bit of advice to summarize his philosophy: "Use it or lose it!"

Leo Musberger

"What you see is what you get."

Computer user's aphorism

MONTANA

Leo Musberger

As we drove into Missoula, Montana, we knew at a glance that we would find our Montana chapter in *this* town and that he (or she) would be a health nut.

It seemed to us that Missoula reeked with an energizing atmosphere and opportunities to enjoy it with health and vigor. We saw swimmers, horseback riders, fishermen, mountain climbers, bikers, tennis players, river rafters, golfers, and roller bladers.

Instinctively, we headed for the West Montana Fitness Center, seeking a retired body personifying Montana fitness. The insightful health club receptionist must have been on our wavelength, because she immediately comprehended our unusual request for a perfect retired specimen and introduced him to us by phone. Later we followed her directions to the foot of a small mountain, where Leo Musberger lives alone in his neat, sunny bungalow.

Leo admits with no apology that staying healthy and fit—and prodding others to do the same—is the focus of his retirement years. Evidence of his personal success are these credentials: at the age of 84 he stands an erect 5' 9", weighs 168 pounds, has a 35" waist, walks briskly with no limp, and, according to his doctor, has the body of a 45 year old man.

Leo let me thump his chest to prove that he is for real. As if that were not convincing enough, he politely but firmly brushed us aside when we offered to help carry his exercise bike up the basement steps for a demonstration.

Leo's physical condition is not by accident. He believes in taking care of himself, working hard, not smoking, and practicing moderation in all areas. As a young man he pitched grain, stacked hay, graded roads, washed dishes, clerked in stores, and stocked shelves. Later as a teacher, coach, and school superintendent, Leo demanded that his students apply the same principles of self discipline which he rigidly continues to apply in his own life today.

He is impatient with his contemporaries who refuse to stay healthy and stay alive. "People who don't keep using their bodies are their own worst enemies," he believes. Leo's routine for staying alive and healthy includes golfing (he's tried out 150 courses); swimming and exercising at the fitness center three times a week; biking; and walking three miles a day.

When we foolishly asked if the destination of his three mile walk was the Senior Center, Leo Musberger gave us a withering look and growled, "I never go near that place."

Richard Garner

"Work is the only way to make
life endurable."

Candide, Voltaire

NEBRASKA

Richard Garner

Richard Garner falls into the same category as thousands who have accepted early retirement buy-outs from the companies which employed them for many years . . . and lived to regret it.

Not long after retiring, Dick made the alarming discovery that he had "just loved to get up every morning and go to work!"

"I'll get another job," he cheerfully announced.

Then the roof caved in. As with so many other retired persons who have been gently persuaded to leave successful positions, Dick Garner could find no job in his field of expertise. To use an over-worked cliché, age was against him. There followed a period of deep discouragement during which Dick's self esteem sank to a new low. It is at a time like this that a fellow needs an understanding wife to prop him up, and fortunately Dick has one. Her name is Sharon.

It wasn't the lack of a salary that bothered Dick. It was the fact that his very nature compels him to work, and he revolted at the possibility of sitting down and becoming lazy, as so many of his retired friends had done.

"People who are able to work should go out and find something they like to do, even if they don't get paid for it," is Dick's philosophy. Out he went to find something he liked to do, a job which would make use of his training and experience. At this point in his life, pounding the pavement for a job was truly an exercise in frustration.

At long last he connected with television station KETV in Omaha, Nebraska, on a part-time basis. Today he finds himself in a full time position as director of the television station's consumer information service.

As it happens, Dick knows more than a bit about relating to consumers, having been an installer for the local telephone company for 25 years. The management training he received at the telephone company also helped prepare him for his new opportunity to train and supervise a staff of volunteers.

Operating from a tiny office filled with telephones and bulging file cabinets, Dick and his volunteers answer questions and seek solutions to a myriad of call-in problems including child abuse, scams, housing, unemployment, aging and long term health care. Dick's assignment is not to act as a consumer advocate but as an empathetic ombudsman, establishing contacts and making referrals. Eighty percent of his attempts have happy endings. "It's gratifying!" he exclaims.

Building on the foundation of a former career, Dick Garner has overcome regrets, frustration, and discouragement to establish a brand new life in retirement.

Jim Taylor

"Tomorrow is another day."

Gone With the Wind, Margaret Mitchell

NEVADA

Jim Taylor

We had been barreling down the highway on automatic cruise control for 70 miles through the high desert land of Nevada without passing a car or seeing a live body. Lulled by the warm sun on the roof and the monotonous scenery all around us, we drifted into a trance and once again indulged in a lovely fantasy:

> We would come up over a little hill and there just in front of us on the right side of the road would stand the proverbial bar room of the Old West. It would naturally be called the Outlaw Tavern, and we would stop for a long anticipated Pepsi. Inside the darkened bar room the walls would be lined with one-armed bandits, guarded from on high by mounted deer heads with impressive antlers. A plump, friendly, blond woman would be presiding behind the bar, and on

*one of the nine brass-bottomed bar
stools would be our next chapter—a
venturer from the East who had
retired and headed for Nevada to
dig for gold!*

Sure enough, we came up over a
little hill. There was the Outlaw Tavern, so
we stopped for a Pepsi! There were the
one-armed bandits, the deer heads, the
antlers, the plump, friendly, blond woman
behind the bar. And on one of the bar
stools, *lo and behold*, there was Jim Taylor.
He was everything we had hoped for—
tough, talkative, weather-beaten, eternally
optimistic, shrewd, and dauntless.

Back East, Jim had operated a successful construction company but had become weary of the government sticking its
nose into his business. So he had tied a
backhoe behind his house trailer, hitched
his trailer to a star, and driven into the sunset. As per script, Jim had invited his wife
to come along, but when she declined he
"went on down the trail alone. Life is too
short to waste any time," he reasoned philo-
sophically.

In the years that followed, Jim staked
out a square mile claim on government

land, dug samples of ore, assayed it to determine the gold content, and approached mining companies to contract for mining. "I haven't just sat around and scratched my head," he explains.

Jim lives in his trusty Winnebago high in the hills of Nevada during the winter, and when the snow melts he returns to the flat land and parks it behind the Outlaw Tavern. There he hammers out slabs of quartzite rock and pans small amounts of gold for tourists, thus augmenting his monthly social security check while he waits for the Big One.

"How big will the Big One be?" I ask Jim Taylor cautiously.

"It's gonna be BIG or I walk away."

"And where will you walk?"

"Well, I've heard of this river down in Costa Rica . . . I have friends . . . they say there's a lot of gold . . . I might just go down there and start dredging . . . ."

His eyes take on a dreamy glaze . . . .

Ruth Burt

"All this and heaven too."
Life of Philip Henry, Matthew Henry

NEW HAMPSHIRE

Ruth Burt

They call it Blueberry Hill, but we called it a sneak preview of heaven: the Appalachian mountain home of Ruth and Herm Burt. It was a steep pull up the dirt road leading to a peak overlooking Canterbury, New Hampshire, but no matter. The result was well worth it. Not only did we gasp at the breathtaking view from the top, but we also met a couple who has achieved for themselves a perfect retirement set up: a rustic home personally designed around their individual interests; a secluded but accessible environment (except after a heavy snowfall); challenging pursuits; robust health; and companionship. Add to these positives Ruth Burt's refreshingly unique philosophy of retirement. More on that later.

As we had traveled through the northeastern section of our country, we had come to realize that New England is truly the birthplace of American crafts. Along with that not-too-new bit of knowledge, we also acquired a not-too-original impression of New Englanders: they are serious, self-disciplined, and they most assuredly finish what they start (we thought).

So imagine our surprise and delight when Ruth Burt, a New England craftsperson of the highest rank, declared unashamedly that the best thing about being retired is that you don't have to finish everything you start! (So much for our New England stereotype!)

Ruth has been starting things ever since she was a six year old child hammering horseshoe nails into crude rings. One craft led to another, and as she studied many media she qualified herself to become Director of Standards for the League of New Hampshire Craftsmen. She held the position for 20 years, inspiring artisans toward perfection and encouraging them to *finish what they start.*

Ruth enjoyed her job with the League, but now that she has resigned she is free to experiment, working with metals and wood, dressmaking, creating jewelry, weaving, and quilting.

While Herm Burt pursues his avid interest in art history, geography, and archeology, Ruth Burt practices her own advice to learn a new skill every year.

Always planning more than can possibly be accomplished, she lives fully the life she loves in their hilltop heaven. Her many projects will be completed on her own schedule, when and if she chooses.

Gus Kuhlman

"The music goes round and round
and it comes out here."

The Music Goes Round and Round,
Rod Hodgson, Edward Farley & Michael Riley

NEW JERSEY

Gus Kuhlman

His eyes light up when he talks, and his enthusiasm sparks the most insulated listener. I, who had never given a second thought to record collectors, found myself sitting spellbound on the edge of my chair as Gus Kuhlman described his career as an engineer; his part-time hobby of the past, his full-time occupation today; and the lifetime legacy he will leave to posterity.

Surrounding us in the Kuhlmans' cozy basement studio were three walls completely lined with sheet music and autographed pictures of Louie Armstrong, Lee Wiley, Jack Teagarden, Carol Leigh, Benny Goodman, Barbara Lee, Bobby Hackett, and other notable musicians too numerous to count. A fourth wall and an adjoining room housed tape players, recording equipment, and the thousands of records Gus has been collecting since boyhood.

"He'll always be happy as long as he has his music," says his pretty wife, Theo, perched on a low ottoman watching Gus admiringly. It occurred to me that she must have idolized him with the same expression when she was 15 and he was lead singer in a jazz band playing for her school's sock hops.

In Gus Kuhlman's unbelievably expansive record collection are 6000 78 RPM records from the 1920s and 1930s alone, in addition to many hundreds of 45s, LPs and CDs. The 78s are his specialty, and he researches their origins and cross files their titles according to label, band, and performing artist so that they can be easily located in his reference library. His researched information is also contributed to a massive list circulated among other collectors.

Gus occasionally discovers titles he needs through that same circulated list, but mostly he scouts out junk stores, antique shops and auctions for his treasures.

Often he is called upon to dub a rare arrangement for a radio production or stage show, and sometimes he is invited to entertain groups with music of a by-gone era.

This he loves to do. Not only is it fun to share his hobby, but it is also satisfying to know that the results of his efforts are providing generations to come with his irreplaceable fund of musical knowledge.

And the beat goes on . . . .

Mac and Marilyn Mackaman

"Oh, what a beautiful mornin',
oh, what a wonderful day."

Oklahoma, Oscar Hammerstein II
& Richard Rogers

NEW MEXICO

Marilyn and Mac Mackaman

"How horrible not to have a reason to get up in the morning."

For the couple who spoke these words, no problem. Marilyn and Mac Mackaman have plenty of reasons to get up every morning.

First they give the overnight guests of the El Aztec Motel a friendly goodbye. Then they enjoy breakfast together in their cozy living quarters attached to the motel. The real fun begins as they pull sheets off beds, gather dirty towels, empty trash cans, and vacuum and dust each of the nine motel rooms that had been rented the night before. For relaxation, they do a little book work to assure that operating their small motel is not only fun but profitable.

The routine is familiar to both of the Mackamans, since both of their career jobs had involved working with the public in operating a construction company, a beauty shop, and a larger motel. Now they not only manage a small motel, but they also own it, do most of the work to maintain it, and live on the premises.

Confining? You bet! But counter-balancing the confinement aspect are the advantages of ownership, companionship, a shared sense of purposefulness, and a nice profit, thank you.

When Marilyn and Mac retired a few years back, they felt as though they "had turned a page and it was blank. Nobody had told us what we were supposed to do after we went on all the cruises."

They only knew that they wanted to keep going, hoped to have association with other people, and were determined to stay on their feet! "If we sit down we may start rocking." Forget that!

Would Marilyn and Mac Mackaman recommend motel operating as a second career for all retired couples? Not unless they have had practical experience in motel management and are prepared for the long days and nights of working solely together, they advise. The Mackamans regard their arrangement as a challenge to keep using —not losing—their minds, their bodies, and even their love for one another.

"This is the good life," they say in tandem, "and best of all we have something to do every day!"

And what will happen if it ever seems that they have too much to do every day?

"Oh, well . . . maybe we'll just shut down a few rooms . . . ."

Harold "Hop" Hopkinson

"Under the spreading chestnut tree . . . ."

The Village Blacksmith,
Henry Wadsworth Longfellow

NEW YORK

Harold "Hop" Hopkinson

It may be slightly out of context, but Robert Browning's line, "the last of life, for which the first was made," comes close to explaining Harold "Hop" Hopkinson's joy in his retirement avocation as a blacksmith.

Harold grew up on a farm in the Northeast. Farms need equipment and equipment often needs repairs. So guess who became the farm's repairman? With his father's instruction plus a do-it-yourself method of his own, Harold learned how to weld together broken pieces of metal farm implements for his family and neighbors and eventually to forge iron into tools. What's more, the tools worked!

Years later, at the conclusion of a successful career as a design engineer for Carrier Air Conditioning, Hop's love for creating, combined with a healthy respect for hard physical labor, lead him quite inevitably back to blacksmithing. Harold and his wife, Betty, live in the small upper New York town of Manlius. Both of them are involved in the cultural, church, and literary activities of their community and in efforts to restore and beautify their town.

On weekend treks into the country-side, the Hopkinsons long ago began collecting bargain-priced blacksmithing equipment, and by the time retirement status arrived Hop had set up a small shop in their garage. Now he had no concern about what he would do with the years ahead. He already knew he would reclaim the blacksmithing ability he had acquired in his boyhood and expand it into an enjoyable and productive hobby.

The garage-shop hobbyist soon became a valuable asset to the history-conscious town of Manlius. It happened when an abandoned blacksmith's building, erected in a nearby town in 1850, was donated lock, stock, and anvil to the Manlius Historical Society museum. Hop was promptly enlisted to fire up the forge and rekindle interest in an art all but lost and forgotten.

Foreign and local visitors now smell the smoke and hurry in to investigate. Sometimes they buy one of Harold's original-design trivets, candlesticks, door handles, or brackets. The purchase price goes toward upkeep of the tiny village museum. Occasionally a visitor expresses a desire to become an amateur blacksmith himself, and Harold finds satisfaction in sharing the knowledge that will keep the craft alive.

Often teachers bring their students to see the primitive blacksmithing tools and to watch, spellbound, as Harold heats a piece of iron red hot and then hammers it into a useable object.

It's enough for Harold "Hop" Hopkinson to know that he has demonstrated a page from history. "He'll never quit," says Betty, "Not as long as he can do it. Men who have retired, like Harold, have so much to give to the world. It's a shame when they only play golf."

Ed McLelland

"Laugh and the world laughs with you.
Weep and you weep alone."

Solitude, Ella Wheeler Wilcox

NORTH CAROLINA

Ed McLelland

One person hears a tune in his head and translates it into a piece of music. Another captures a random phrase from the ether and writes a poem. A woman rummages through a bag of rags and stitches a quilt. And then there is Ed McLelland. Ed looks at discarded parts of old tractors lying around in his shop and begins welding.

The results of his welding are a collection of metal conversation starters that defy description. Some are actually artistic, as is the manure-spreader chain frozen in action. Some are recognizable, as are the toy cannons. Some are useful, as are the oversized table lamps. Some are useless, as is the paper weight too heavy to lift. And some are just plain funny, as is Gumbo.

Gumbo is so called because, like chicken gumbo soup, he is a conglomeration of many ingredients. Standing four-and-a-half feet tall, he glitters splendidly in the McLelland trademark of bright gold metallic spray paint. Although two of Gumbo's body parts are a mower seat and a steering wheel, further similarity to anything you've ever seen before is purely coincidental.

Some of Gumbo's other anatomical details began as ring gears, clutch disc, hydraulic piston, diesel piston, lever, and gear shift, but Gumbo doesn't work. He just stands there. The reason is that his fuel injector is disconnected from his fuel pump, Ed explains. (Sure it is, I agree.) "You gotta stay connected," continues the inventor turned philosopher.

"You gotta stay connected to your family and your neighbors and your fellow man. But mostly you gotta stay connected to the Lord."

Ed McLelland's creations are usually humorous, because Ed himself is a man of humor. He laughs easily at his own jokes as well as at ours, and his determination to keep laughing and keep working has paid off in the not-so-good times along the way.

When his career ended and he retired as manager and president of a Ford tractor sales and service agency near Statesville in North Carolina, it was financially necessary that Ed supplement a social security check to cover mounting medical bills. (Ed's wife, Mildred, is seriously handicapped by arthritis, and Ed has experienced open heart surgery.) Naturally he turned to the work he knows best: repairing broken tractors and other farm equipment in his backyard workshop which he dubbed, *"el Spirito de Tractorino Farmo."*

In the garage, repaired machines stand waiting to be picked up by their owners. Broken and replaced tractor parts which Ed "can't stand to throw away" lie in neat piles awaiting their metamorphosis.

After stumbling awkwardly into a rejuvenated metal Viking (just my size) in full battle array, I hardly dared to ask what the next creation would be. Ed McLelland doesn't know yet, but take his word for it, he already has it in his mind, and for sure "it's gonna be right pretty."

Don Voss

"This life . . . is what we make it."

The Will to Believe, William James

NORTH DAKOTA

Don Voss

If you can no longer do what you once did, then do what you *can* do *now*. But don't give up!

These words did not actually come from the mouth of Don Voss, but they express in a simple way the philosophy his life exemplifies so eloquently.

During all of his adult career, Don had worked as a cabinet maker and carpenter. Not your ordinary hammer and saw carpenter, mind you, but a craftsman. A perfectionist. An artist. The beautiful house he built to share with his wife, Grace, and the many pieces of turned wood that furnish it are evidences of his talent.

So it was a hard pill to swallow when doctors diagnosed in Don the discouraging symptoms of Parkinson's disease. Don was well aware of the illness's prognosis. There would be a gradual deterioration in certain nerve centers of the brain, and more than likely he would lose much of the fine muscle control that guided his woodworking.

Did Don hang up his craftsman's tools and settle into an attitude of self pity? Not on your life!

Instead, inspired by a Tiffany lamp in his living room, he decided to become a stained glass artist while there was yet time. Not only would he learn this new skill, but he would reinforce his knowledge by teaching it to other students—45 of them within a two year period.

Don knew that the months when his hand would follow his exact bidding were limited. But when the Voss's church in the little town of Bowman, North Dakota, approached him to design, fabricate, and install ten 22 by 90 inch stained glass windows in the sanctuary, he quickly agreed and freely devoted his full-time effort to the project.

The magnificent windows and the stories behind them now inspire the congregation Sunday after Sunday. As for Don Voss, he still refuses to give in to the debilitating disease which rerouted his direction. As his fine muscle skills diminish, Don relies more on his gross muscles to continue to create beauty for the world in other forms.

(Remember: If you can no longer do what you once did, then do what you *can* do *now*. But don't give up!)

Robert Guion

"A scholar knows no boredom."

Hesperus, Jean Paul Richter

OHIO

Robert Guion

Bowling Green, Ohio, is the home of a large, thriving university. It is also near the center of the glass blowing industry in Toledo. These two geographical tidbits are thrown in (for free) to suggest that the environment one lives in must surely influence a person's choice of career, avocation, attitude, and retirement pursuits.

Take Dr. Robert Guion as an example. Robert is an educator by profession, a former industrial psychology professor. Currently he is an advisor on doctoral dissertations, author, editor of a journal on applied psychology, and expert on fair employment issues. These are the interesting pursuits that linger from his teaching days.

But in line with his determination to never allow himself to become bored, Robert Guion has taken advantage of the glass blowing industry which surrounds him and has become an excellent glass blower in his own right. Periodically, he reinforces his self-taught method by attending classes in glass blowing at Bowling Green University, and he spends hours each week experimenting with unique effects in glass. We visited him in the basement studio of his comfortable home and were filled with admiration for the beauty of his original glass creations.

While Robert has tangible results to display from his glass blowing avocation, some of his other ventures are less visible to his guests. "Take up something new every year," he advises retirees. "If you like it, you'll keep it up, whether it's glass blowing, flying, golfing, farming, or even playing the bassoon."

Surrounded by a circle of former professors, friends who are also developing and using their talents in retirement, Robert Guion is modest about his own accomplishments. To us, however, any retired person is remarkable who can say, as Robert does, "I've *never* had to ask, 'what am I going to do now?'"

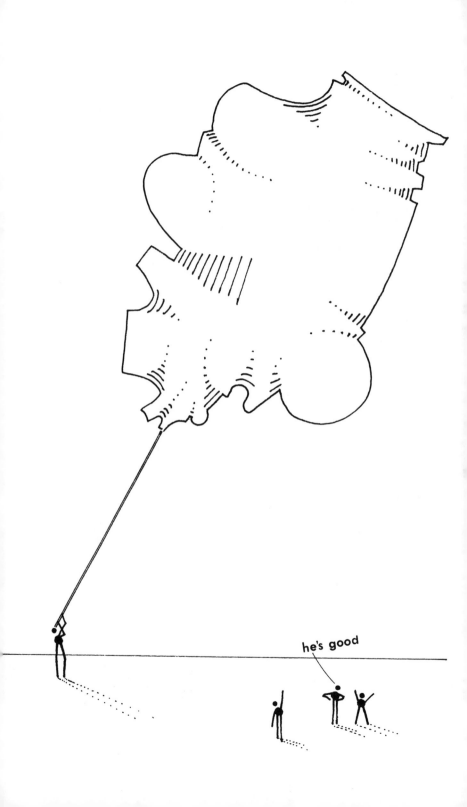

Nadine Fontaine

"This is the day . . . let us rejoice
and be glad in it."
Psalm 118:24 (Revised Standard Version)

OKLAHOMA

Nadine Fontaine

When Nadine Fontaine's husband, Oscar, died, Nadine could have retired comfortably as the respected widow of a well known Oklahoma Methodist pastor. Instead she enrolled at Southern Methodist University and prepared herself to carry on his ministry for a while. "Grief is a part of living," she says, "but when you lose your mate you must go on, not to forget, but to remember."

When Nadine retired as a minister, herself, she could have sat back and lived comfortably on the investment income from a modest inheritance. Instead she bought a beauty shop (still finding time, of course, for church and civic responsibilities and for counseling battered women).

It just so happened that a restaurant went up for sale at the precise moment Nadine retired as a beauty shop operator. "I had never been in the restaurant business before, so I decided to give it a fling," she explains logically.

The "fling" seems to be succeeding beautifully. We visited with Nadine at "Mi Patio," her cozy, attractively decorated restaurant tucked away in the mini-mall which meanders through the downtown section of Miami, Oklahoma. Nadine supervises her five employees, does all the buying and bookkeeping, and in general oversees the establishment.

"Make the most of the talent you've been given," she says, referring to her business ability and college training.

When Nadine underwent a mastectomy for breast cancer a few years ago, she could have retired with the justification of ill health. Instead she cried vigorously for two seconds, then energetically began squeezing a ball for exercise. "I had to have a good arm so I could carry my suitcase when I went to Africa," she points out.

What happens next? Nadine Fontaine isn't sure, but she isn't worried. The reason is that every morning when she wakes up, her first question is, "Lord, what are we going to do today?"

She gives God a few minutes to answer. And then she hops out of bed and gets started.

Otis and Goldie Hickman

"We'll travel the road,
sharing our load,
side by side."

Side By Side, Harry Woods

OREGON

Goldie and Otis Hickman

Appropriately dressed in matching western outfits, they met us at the town museum, eager to share with us the product of their togetherness. Their "togetherness" and the results of it turned out to be equally impressive.

Goldie and Otis Hickman have built, and are continuing to build, a 19th century western town constructed meticulously to scale, approximately one eighth inch to one foot. ("We call it the Hickman scale—when we both agree it's right.")

It all started one day when Otis looked at a child's small Wells Fargo bank and decided to hack out a stage coach to stand in front of it. He had so much fun that, when he retired as an employee of the local gas company, he continued to whittle because a dream was beginning to take form: why not whittle a whole town?

At this point some wives might have nagged their husbands with, "Why don't you do something useful with your time?" Instead, Goldie Hickman asked, "What can I do to help?"

As the project developed, Otis emerged as the artist, visionary, the perfectionist carver, and Goldie as the encourager, the praiser, the stitcher, the finder of small lost parts. Together they search through magazines, history books and encyclopedias to assure that each piece is historically authentic.

So far the small western town replica includes boarding house, general store, barber shop, two windmills, livery stable, the Horse Shoe Cafe, sheriff's office, covered wagon, sheep herder's wagon, gun and saddle shop, toboggan, canoes, sleds, and an outhouse complete with a miniature Sears Roebuck catalog.

For construction material, Otis garners old siding, broken picket fences, tomato plant support poles, cottonwood bark, discarded leather for tiny saddles and bridles, metal from an ancient space heater, copper tubing, and anything that looks useable. From the most unlikely sources he creates the buildings and furnishings, tools, utensils, and equipment, down to a minute shaving mug on the shelf of a covered wagon.

On the whittler's agenda are a church, a school, and as many homes as are needed for the unpredictable population of "River's Bend, fantasy village of the 19th century West." In the meantime, tourists and the townspeople of Pendleton, Oregon, enjoy a rare peek at history being reconstructed in exacting detail in front of their very eyes.

River's Bend may never be totally complete, but that's all right with Goldie and Otis Hickman. Their unfinished symphony coincides with their philosophy: "Find something you love and stay with it."

Joseph and Dorothy McFerron

"Off we go, into the wild blue yonder."

Air Force Song

PENNSYLVANIA

Dorothy and Joseph McFerron

Meeting Dorothy and Joseph McFerron in New Stanton, Pennsylvania, added an unexplored dimension to the subject of retirement. Here are two persons who not only are succeeding in staying on their feet, retaining close ties with their family, serving their community, and helping others, but they are also helping others in third world countries to help themselves. In that capacity, they have become unofficial ambassadors of the United States.

Sound like a pretty large assignment? You're right, but the McFerrons insist it is within the realm of possibility for any retired executive, male or female, who has the desire to share what he or she knows with a struggling business or agency overseas.

The McFerrons' expertise is in the field of medicine and hospital administration. Before retiring, Joe was director of a community health center and Dottie was a school nurse. Following the first commandment for happy retirement, they began planning ahead long before the Big Day arrived.

Their plan involved listing their names with the International Executive Service Corps. This organization recruits executive and technical advisors to volunteer their know-how and experience on a short-term basis with people in developing nations who request business assistance.

Dottie and Joe's first three-month assignment was to help a hospital in Ecuador formulate plans for a modern facility. Later, they were sent to Jamaica where they and their corps team made recommendations for improvement at a large hospital in Kingston.

While we were contented to relax in the charm of their Pennsylvania home one sunny morning, both Dottie and Joe were champing at the bit to leave again for Jamaica. They had already been accepted for another three-month stint there and are looking forward to assignments in other parts of the world when a need arises.

Ugly Americans? Not Dottie and Joe McFerron.

These are beautiful Americans who have skills to offer and refuse to see them waste away from lack of exercise.

Ralph aRusso

"I did it my way."

I Did It My Way, Paul Anka

RHODE ISLAND

Ralph aRusso

Once, in our quest for retired self-starters with a focus for their lives, our unorthodox method of discovering said persons landed us more than we had bargained for. No complaint!

Specifically, in Johnston, Rhode Island, we marched boldly into City Hall, and, as we explained our unusual request to the receptionist, a tall, handsome, white haired man standing nearby cordially invited us into his office.

Not until we were firmly established facing our host across his massive desk did we realize that we were in the presence of The Great One himself, The Mayor!

We did not get up and leave!

Although it was not our practice to seek out celebrities to interview, this one was too good to pass up. After all, were we not innocently sitting in his office through no effort of our own? And how else would we ever learn how a public official feels when he reaches retirement age and chooses to ignore it?

Ralph aRusso did just that. After serving eleven two-year terms as mayor of Johnston, he was recently re-elected and is looking forward to running again. And again. And again. "And why not?" he asks. "I don't want to stop being mayor as long as I'm healthy. I want to work. All of us have 24 hours in the day, and we ought to make the most of them, not just lie on the couch and watch television." (Ah—mayor or not, here was a man after our own hearts.) "Besides, I feel I have a lot to contribute, and I even think I have an obligation to contribute it," the mayor continues.

We were so carried away by Ralph aRusso's forthrightness and hospitality that we totally neglected to ask him the 64 dollar question before we floated out of his office on a cloud of joy. Undaunted, we dashed immediately into the nearest roadside phone booth and called him.

"Mayor aRusso," I panted breathlessly, ". . . forgot to ask . . . what advice can you give other retired persons who want to be public servants . . . like you . . . ?"

His answer was characteristically quick and practical. "Start at the level you're on now—maybe a parent teacher organization or charitable program. Get yourself appointed to a committee, then to a board. *Keep your name in front of the public.* Finally, run for an office on the town council. If you win the election, you'll be on your way."

(Author's note: You'll be more likely to win if you add a little "a" in front of your name. That will put you alphabetically at the top of the ballot on election day! It's legitimate and it worked for Mayor aRusso!)

Wini Meachen

"(S)he is well paid that is well satisfied."
The Merchant of Venice, William Shakespeare

SOUTH CAROLINA

Wini Meachen

"I was bored," Wini Meachen stated bluntly.

We glanced around the handsome living room and through the windows at the sculptured lawns beyond and thought to ourselves: if we had to be bored, Hilton Head Island, South Carolina, wouldn't be too shabby a place to be bored in.

The Meachen family relocated from Hawaii, where Wini's husband, Donald, was stationed for 24 years as a civilian engineer with the United States Army. They bought a beautiful golf course home on luxurious Hilton Head Island and anticipated settling down to a life of comfort and leisure.

It was the *leisure* part that was too much for Wini.

Golf and tennis and swimming and bridge were fine for a while, but Wini was as restless as a willow in a wind storm and she needed an outlet for her creative energies.

Coming from a background of art, Wini had always enjoyed painting and doing crafts. So when she began looking around for a meaningful activity to fill her many available hours, she naturally gravitated toward something artistic that she could do with her hands.

Wini had gathered a few interesting stones in her travels, and these stones now inspired her to experiment in jewelry making. She was so excited by the results that she soon branched out and familiarized herself with various jewelry styles and sources of materials. Today she speaks knowledgeably of dyed lapis, ivory, blue onyx, hand carved bone, diamond cut silver, and hematite.

Although Hilton Head Island is a mecca for vacationers, Wini's jewelry is definitely not of the souvenir variety. The cost of her carefully selected materials unfortunately dictates the price of her one-of-a-kind pieces. Monetary success *would* be nice, but, as with all true artists, it is the least of Wini Meachen's concerns. She creates beautiful necklaces, earrings, bracelets and pins for the pure joy of creating and sharing.

Lucky her family and friends at Christmas time!

Duane Friese

"What do we live for if it is not to make life
less difficult for each other?"

Author unknown

SOUTH DAKOTA

Duane Friese

Rodeos are big in the high plains of South Dakota, so we were not surprised to encounter a retired rodeo performer as the South Dakota entry in our book.

His name is Duane Friese, and, although he never risked life and limb on a bucking bronco, he entertained audiences all along the circuit as the rodeo clown. Making people happy is what it's all about anyway, according to this genial man with the contagious laugh.

When he retired from the rodeo, it was his desire to spread happiness that led Duane to his present position as house manager of Hickory House retirement home in Spearfish, South Dakota. Duane had often observed that people are treated badly as they grow older, and he didn't like it. Everyone needs to feel loved, he reasoned. Everyone needs to keep laughing, no matter what his or her age.

As a retirement home manager, he

could fill those needs. Here was a job that was made to order for Duane Friese, but in no way is he your ordinary retirement house manager. He plants flowers in the spring-time, carries trays for the frail, and gets up in the night to sweep the snow off the side-walks. All of the residents are "his people," and they respond to him affectionately as their "house daddy."

Duane gives his people love, and he also provides them with plenty of laughs. On impulse, he often dons his familiar ro-deo clown suit and goes into his act. Pres-ently, he is learning to play the piano so that he can entertain in the dining room and accompany congregational singing at in-house church services.

On very special occasions, Duane cranks up his ancient jalopy (tastefully color coordinated to his clown suit) and takes "the girls" out to dinner in Spearfish.

Duane doesn't drink or smoke and he makes no apology for "living for Christ," which for him obviously includes the Golden Rule. When he has to quit, he says, he hopes and prays someone will treat him the way he's trying to treat his people: he calls them all by name, but he never calls them "old."

Jim Cortese

"Don't fence me in."

Don't Fence Me In, Cole Porter

TENNESSEE

Jim Cortese

Some people write because writing is their job. Jim Cortese writes because he has a compulsion to write, and since he also has a compulsion to be an adventurer, he obviously has plenty to write about. What a convenient combination of compulsions!

Jim enjoyed a long, successful career as a small town newspaper editor, a large city newspaper columnist, and a published book author. But if Jim had followed any other line of work he undoubtedly would still have written. Only those who are fired with that same insatiable need to write can understand its urgency.

During his professional years, Jim drew from limitless sources for his subject material. Today he is most often inspired by his own experiences, which are also limitless.

Some of his adult escapades include swimming the Mississippi and, on another occasion, paddling a canoe the full length of that same river; playing Beethoven's Fifth Symphony full blast on a turntable from the depths of the Grand Canyon; roller skating across the state of Texas; climbing the steps to the top of the Empire State building; reciting the Gettysburg address from the site of its original delivery; driving the highway to Alaska four times; making regular winter fishing trips to Mexico; and hiking the Appalachian trail from Georgia to Maine.

Achieving retirement status has not altered Jim's philosophical convictions. "Life is meant to be enjoyed," he says with emphasis. "Just because you're retired doesn't mean you have to stop *living*. Retirement is when you have *time* to *enjoy* it."

On the day of our visit in his Tennessee home, Jim Cortese didn't know what his next venture would be, but "We're sure going to do something. We're not just going to sit down and die!"

The Cortese trailer and Jim's trusty typewriter stand by in a constant state of preparedness. Equally on the alert is his ever-ready wife, Anne, who is convinced that her husband can do anything—and probably will.

Helen Jordan

"Nothing great was ever achieved
without enthusiasm."

Circles, Ralph Waldo Emerson

TEXAS

Helen Jordan

She was tall, attractive, and vibrantly alive as she bounded across the parking lot of the Denny's restaurant in Baytown, Texas, where we had agreed to meet. Later over lunch, we added "enthusiastic" to the list of our first impressions of Helen Jordan.

Enthusiasm big time is what Helen has plenty of, and it's the quality she wishes for everyone else. "Retire as soon as you can and start having fun," she recommends. "Unless you're having fun now!"

Having fun is synonymous with being excited, in Helen's vocabulary, and "Everybody needs to be excited about something!"

Following her own advice, Helen stopped working in her long-time career job with a large oil company when she was offered an early retirement buy-out. She immediately began having fun.

Fun for her eventually became a new career.

Helen had long been interested in physical fitness, having dealt with several injuries in her family. She had also encountered problems of work-related stress pain in her position as an insurance clerk, and she had observed that many of her co-workers faced retirement ill-prepared physically.

Soon after retiring, Helen became aware of the fairly new medically related muscle and exercise technique known as "myotherapy." Helen saw the pressure-massage-stretch procedure of myotherapy as a viable method of relieving muscular pain and restoring mobility in older people, athletes, and musicians, among others. She determined to become a skilled technician. With her "won't quit" supply of energy, she tackled a two year training course and was awarded full certification as a myotherapist. Now she enthusiastically contributes to the well-being of many while she builds an exciting life for herself.

Her new career is not only fun, it is lucrative. "So what's wrong with making money?" Helen Jordan laughingly asks.

and stretch

Lela Gubler

"Get a life."

Author unknown

UTAH

Lela Gubler

If you're a grandmother and think there's nothing ahead for you but sitting in a rocking chair, meet Lela Gubler of Hurricane, Utah.

Lela had been a waitress in other people's cafes off and on since she was 15. In her words, she always liked "slinging hash, meeting people and having a dollar in my pocket." Of course, she had taken frequent timeouts to raise her three children, help her husband, Kay, on the farm, and nurse numerous relatives through serious illnesses.

When the child raising and the nursing eventually came to an end, Lela took a long look into the future. It was not a pretty picture: "You can clean, you can cook, you can wash the clothes, then you can flop down and watch TV."

But such a life was not for Lela.

She was homesick for the friendly sounds of customers enjoying a good meal. She yearned to meet new people and be part of the action. She missed the satisfaction of being told she was a terrific cook.

Lela made a decision. She would open a little restaurant in her home and call it "Grandma's Country Kitchen (Where Grandma Cooks With Love)." She would feature all the recipes she knew best— home made noodles in chicken soup, home made pies and cakes and sweet rolls; chicken fried steak; biscuits and gravy; breakfast all day long; and, of course, *real* mashed potatoes.

To other grandmothers who aspire to independence, Lela says, "Get out and do something with your life." For Lela it only meant overcoming the objections of her family, getting permission from the town fathers, buying equipment, clearing out her yard for parking spaces, and tearing down the wall between her bedroom, utility room, and family room!

Nothing to it, if you're Lela Gubler. As for the rewards, "If I died tomorrow I'd be happier than if I hadn't done it, because I found out I could do something on my own."

Walter and Virginia Truslow and Ruth Conrad

"Whoever is happy will make
others happy, too"

The Diary of a Young Girl, Anna Frank

VERMONT

Virginia and Walter Truslow and Ruth Conrad

At the Truslow home in Vermont, retirement is a family affair.

There, in a spacious house filled with priceless old quilts, dried flowers, original paintings, and antique furniture, live Virginia Truslow (better known as Ginny), a former art teacher; her husband, Walter (better known as Ted), also a former headmaster and teacher; and Ginny's mother, Ruth Conrad, known affectionately as Ruth.

After Ginny retired from teaching a few years ago, she discovered that she was finally free to do the work she wanted to do. She could try her hand at designing in fabric—a dream she had harbored for years. She could create quilts and make dolls and teddy bears without constant interruptions. Most importantly, she constantly reminded herself, she would no longer waste precious hours on things she didn't really enjoy.

Ginny's manager, agent, bookkeeper, and right hand man is Ted, a crafts enthusiast in his own right. Ted's pride in his wife's skills is matched only by his desire to keep himself busy working with Ginny and participating in church, civic and music endeavors.

Just around the corner in an adjoining room during our visit was 96 year old Ruth, busily stuffing cotton into unattached body parts of future dolls and bears. "I don't mind, it keeps me busy," she says, fully in tune with the philosophy of her co-workers.

It was Ruth who long ago first taught her little girl, Ginny, to sew. And today, at another stage of all of their lives, mother and daughter, along with son-in-law and husband Ted, design, stitch, and market their wonderful crafts.

The marketing process involves selling their productions at a local crafts cooperative shop they help operate. They also participate in nine or ten craft shows each year. These efforts subsidize their income significantly.

In some situations, three may be a crowd, but in the Truslow-Conrad household it's a happy trio—individually investing

their talents and collectively reaping divi-
dends of satisfaction.

Jane Elizabeth Atkinson

"I am the master of my fate;
. . . the captain of my soul."

Invictus, William Henry Henley

VIRGINIA

Jane Elizabeth Atkinson

"I got tired of being dumped on." That flat-out declaration of independence from perky Jane Elizabeth Atkinson emphatically sums up her frank reaction to a situation thousands of men and women find themselves in soon after they stop working at their career jobs.

The demands that triggered Jane's rebellion are familiar to all persons newly retired: "I know you have time on your hands" . . . "now that you're not working" . . . "we need you at the library" . . . "the hospital" . . . "the school" . . . "the homeless" . . . "the church" . . . "one hour here" . . . "two hours there" . . . "it's only one day a week . . . "

It so happens that Jane believes in all these causes, and she soon found herself dashing pell-mell between many of them, trying to "do her part." In a very short time, she discovered that by answering "yes" to every request for her volunteer efforts she had ceased to control her life and itinerary. She had lost her focus.

As former director of a section of the Clinical Chemistry Department at the Medical College of Virginia, Jane was accustomed to planning her days, scheduling appointments, working with people, zeroing in on a goal, meeting deadlines, exerting self discipline. She was comfortable with her role, and when her role changed, she became frustrated.

Jane hit bottom, bounced, and came up knowing exactly what was needed to give her life structure once again: a part-time job where she could use the attributes which had qualified her for a successful career, one in which she would meet and serve many people, and one which would offer regular hours. If she were paid a salary, all the better!

Eventually Jane joined the staff of the Metropolitan Richmond Visitor Center. Geographically and historically, she knows the area and its people and is well prepared to share her lifetime knowledge with visitors. On occasion, she even personally guides sightseers to local places of interest.

Jane has not totally abandoned her volunteer pursuits—in fact, on the day we met she was at her church helping to herd members of the congregation through the intricate maze of their annual picture-taking routine. Tomorrow, though, she'll be back at the Metropolitan Richmond Visitor Center. Definite hours. Definite duties. And definite structure.

Jane Elizabeth Atkinson will be in control of her life.

And that's definite!

Bill VanBeek

"A man's best friend is his dog."

Author Unknown

WASHINGTON

Bill VanBeek

When Bill VanBeek retired from his United States Corps of Engineers position, he stated emphatically, "From now on I won't do anything for money. I'm going to work on my own schedule."

This was a long speech for Bill, because, by his own admission, he doesn't talk much.

Also by his own admission, he doesn't enjoy socializing. On the other hand, Bill is public spirited and has a sincere desire to serve humanity with his newly acquired free time.

Now how in the world was this quiet, unassuming man going to find an outlet for his love and altruistic motives?

Enter Banjo.

Banjo is a dog. A golden retriever, to be exact.

Banjo had been trained as a seeing eye dog, but later she was rejected because of a slight hip impairment. However, she is beautiful, otherwise healthy and well-mannered, and her nature is as outgoing as Bill's is retiring.

Together they are a combination made in heaven.

Enter Elizabeth, Bill's wife. No jealousy here, just a loving desire to contribute to the retirement career of the happy couple, Bill and Banjo. Elizabeth sews when she isn't volunteering at the YWCA nursery or in the hospital gift shop. Her specialty is creating canine *chappeaus,* and 30 of these she has custom made for Banjo, who wears them with individuality and flair.

Now Bill and Banjo spend many hours each week gathering smiles and spreading joy wherever they go. Their main destination is St. Mary Hospital in their home town of Walla Walla, Washington. They stroll the hallways greeting visitors, and, because of Banjo's impeccable behavior, stylish headgear, and charm, they are often invited into patients' rooms.

Visiting the hospital is not their only activity, however. Bill and Banjo also march in parades, cheer at Little League games, attend dinners, and drop in on school picnics.

Always they are welcome guests who add to the occasion just by being who they are: Banjo the entertainer, Bill the straight man.

"Now I don't have to socialize," says Bill, "Banjo does it for me."

But Bill and Banjo both know it takes two to tango.

John Kounse

"I hear music when I look at you."

The Song Is You, Oscar Hammerstein II
& Jerome Kern

WEST VIRGINIA

John Kounse

John Kounse sat at the old Steinway in his living room, stretching and massaging his painfully arthritic hands. Finally, with a small sigh of resignation, he began playing, tentatively at first, experimenting with the 10-note rolled bass chord that had once driven his wife, Mary Louise, crazy as he pushed for perfection.

As his gnarled fingers gradually lost their stiffness, John began to really roll those bass chords, and then with his right hand he added the melody of "Sweetheart of Sigma Chi," "Shanty in Old Shanty Town," and his favorite, "Memories."

John Kounse has plenty of them. Memories, that is. He remembers his mother, a pianist and piano teacher, standing over him at the piano when he was a little boy. He remembers the proverbial broomstick in her hand and the dreaded admonition on her lips, "Practice . . . or else . . . ."

John admired his mother's technical skill but rebelled at being taught only the classical selections she preferred. His education in music thus ended abruptly, soon after it began. If he had been allowed to play jazz instead, he muses, ah—how different things might have been. To this very day John believes, with a twinge of regret, that he could have had a successful career as pianist in a Dixieland jazz band.

But when he was growing up, most parents were not sending their young men out into the world to become ragtime musicians. Their ambition centered more on such respectable professions as shoe salesman, factory worker, or wholesale produce distributor.

John reluctantly conformed and followed these diverse pursuits for the bulk of his adult life, while his foot tapped a secret rhythm and his fingers itched to touch a piano keyboard and bring forth the sound of the music in his head.

When he stopped working, the day finally came when John had time to play to his heart's content. A jazz musician friend gave him a few lessons, but mostly John is self-taught by the trial and error method, and he plays entirely by ear. When he makes an occasional flub, his family and friends say, "So what! Not many 88-year-olds, eaten up with arthritis, play at all!"

John wishes everyone would learn to play an instrument, at least enough to have fun at it, even if they begin late in life. He may not be able to hunt and fish and golf and "gig" frogs, as he did in the early years of his retirement, but he still has his music and, as John says, "Music is like food. It fills you up."

Music also fills the halls of the Elks Club several times a week when John entertains his fellow members. "And if you happen to come back this way sometime, and the night is right, I'll play again for you," he promised us.

It's a date, John Kounse.

Thelma Marasek

"You're never too old to learn."

The Mayor of Quinborough,
Thomas Middleton

WISCONSIN

Thelma Marasek

Thelma Marasek is a high school dropout. Her mother, a teacher, pleaded with her to stay in school and get her diploma. But Thelma has a stubborn nature, and she defiantly left home at the age of 16 to make her way in the big city. Today Thelma lives alone in an upstairs apartment with her memories . . . and her regrets.

Correction: Thelma Marasek WAS a high school dropout. Her mother DID plead with her to stay in school. She DID, eventually, follow her mother's wishes to get an education, and because she HAS such a stubborn nature she DID get her high school diploma—*at the age of 86!* Thelma DOES live alone in an upstairs apartment with her memories (and her cat), but she has NO REGRETS because she knows, at last, that her mother would be proud of her.

Thelma received her General Equivalency Diploma after four years of study through the Chippewa Valley Technical

College, with encouragement from the Phillips Senior Central of Eau Claire, Wisconsin. "Yes, it was a challenge," she admits. "In fact, the last two exams were pure hell, if you want me to put it in the vernacular." (We did, and she did).

Her efforts were definitely worth it, because she says that no longer will she feel inferior or left out at her class reunions!

Thelma is something of a celebrity in Eau Claire these days. Although she modestly claims not to know what all the hoopla is about, she is proud of her accomplishment and is determined to set a fire under some of her contemporaries.

"It's a pity people think they can't learn just because they're old," she says.

"Old" is certainly not a term you would apply to Thelma. True, she freely shares recollections of other years: a happy marriage, travels, and employment as a nurse's assistant, motel maid, crossing guard, and factory worker. But Thelma lives in the present. Alone and independent, she takes care of herself and her apartment, and both are neat and attractive. Although the near future holds an eye implant and a foot operation, on the day of our visit she was more concerned about her plans to set out her tomato plants as soon as we left.

Here is a lady with a mission in life to convince others that, "You're not through when you're a senior citizen."

Emily Toth

"Where there's a will, there's a way."

Author unknown

WYOMING

Emily Toth

Emily Toth knew what she wanted and she knew how to get it. That's why this attractive divorcee of retirement age is where she is today: happy, employed, and fulfilled.

She wanted to continue working as long as her health permitted. She did!

When cancer knocked her down, she determined to fight it with all her vigor. She won!

When her kids settled her in a senior citizen highrise apartment, she decided it wasn't for her. She rebelled!

When she realized that the West Coast was too congested for her peace of mind, she moved to the wide open spaces of Wyoming.

But after establishing herself in a comfortable mobile home, Emily faced the fact that sitting in a rocker watching TV wasn't exactly what she had in mind for her future. She turned off the TV and analyzed the situation.

Emily is a people person. She wanted a social life. She wanted to feel needed. She wanted to work.

But how to get a dream job in Sheridan, Wyoming, where openings for women are scarce. For women who are but don't think of themselves as senior citizens, jobs are virtually non-existent. Emily finally resorted to seeking help from the local Senior Employment Services of AARP, and the program proved to be a God-send.

Evelyn was placed for on-the-job training in the WYO Theater box office. She was so enthusiastic, learned so readily, and made herself so indispensable that she was eventually offered the permanent position of box office manager.

The WYO Theatre is the cultural center of Sheridan—the setting for community concerts, dance recitals, touring companies, jazz bands, performers in every field. It's the setting Emily craves. As daytime reservationist, she meets townspeople and visitors alike. At night she slips into a snazzy black and white outfit and greets guests at the box office or in the theater lobby.

To say that Emily Toth is in seventh heaven is an understatement. This woman knows what it means to catch a falling star and put it in her pocket . . . and never let it go!

THE LAST WORD

Two years, 50 states, 43,694 miles, 81 motels and 309 fast food restaurants ago, we began our journey of discovery. (These figures are validated in the "Jim French Little Black Book of Expense Records.")

There were short trips out from our home base in Dundee, Illinois; long trips across the continent; postponed trips; and interrupted trips. Always the trips were interspersed with family, church, community and home responsibilities. Always they were fun and made with a single purpose: to locate a self-starter in each state who has personally found a time-consuming, satisfying focus for his or her life in the years following a career job.

How did you discover these people, you ask? We merely used every single method that entered our fertile brains: radar, instinct, persistence, and just plain luck. We were bolder than we had ever imagined ourselves to be.

Only four times did we have pre-arranged introductions. In every other instance we were on our own, and "our own" consisted of randomly pin-pointing a town on the map, driving to it, parking the car, saying a quick prayer, getting out, and gabbing.

We talked to store clerks, firemen, newspaper editors, radio and TV station operators, school and college officials, waitresses, ministers, librarians, gas station attendants, government workers, hospital personnel, and others too numerous to list.

All of the people we appealed to for recommendations were cordial and helpful. Moreover, they seemed to be pleased to have a representative of their area included in a book. If we talked long enough, eventually we gleaned the name of a person who would definitely fit our very high criteria as to personality, philosophy, and "focus."

From there on out, it was easy going. A telephone call usually cinched an appointment for an interview, if for no other reason than the interviewee was curious about the whacko couple named Ginny and Jim French who had dropped out of the blue (Chevrolet) into their lives.

Then came the joy of really becoming acquainted, one at a time, with the personalities in the profiles you have just read. Although all of them would claim that their lives are not spectacular, we can attest to the fact that they are most assuredly *distinctive*.

As we traveled across the United States, encountering many people no longer in the work force, we became more and more convinced of the ugly truth we had heretofore suspected: there *is* a retirement trap, and the trap is set for all of us by an age-conscious society, together with the set of inevitable circumstances that accompanies retirement.

Consider, for example, the circumstance of excess leisure time. Many retired couples, like ourselves, live on a pension check, Social Security, and returns from investments, so no longer are we impelled to hold a job, scurry to appointments, earn a salary. Diabolically, a situation which should generate relaxation and contentment, contributes instead to the reality of the dreaded retirement trap. As the urgency to make interesting plans and follow tight sched-ules disappears, inertia takes over, and all too soon we find ourselves drifting aimlessly across a dreary plateau of inactivity. We regard a day as eventful if we do only one small act that is out of the ordinary. Time loses its significance, and our creature comforts become the end-all of our existence: sleeping late, dressing, eating, keep-ing warm, taking a nonstrenuous walk, napping, eating, watching a little television, and going back to bed. Unfortunately, this dull pattern coincides *precisely* with the world's uncompli-mentary perception of the routine of older people.

We believe, however, that most of us do not choose to be listless, bored, and uninterest-ing in the "fourth quarter" of life's game. Many of us do not even choose to retire but *allow* ourselves to *be retired*, to be benched, as it were, while the game goes on without us. Our youth-centered culture, with the media as its promoter, fosters low expectations of the pro-ductive ability and even physical appearance of retirees. And we too often obligingly comply by becoming *unproductive* and by prematurely adopting the unappealing, tell-tale characteristics of the very old. We lean forward, hunch our shoulders, frequently refer to our health deficiencies, melt down into our waistlines, move ever more slowly, and shuffle as we walk—long before we need to.

If we manage to sidestep the retirement trap, our after-career years can be joyous ones. If we fall into the trap, we permit ourselves to become stereotypical "retirees" in the most derogatory sense of the word.

The retirement trap is so insidious that only with the greatest determination can we stay clear of it and continue to be the vital persons we planned to be when we reached this stage. *The individuals or couples we interviewed innately anticipated the trap, and it was their determination to avoid it that convinced us they have something to teach the rest of us.*

To describe one of these self-starters is to describe them all, because, amazingly, they have so many qualities in common. Their individual personalities seem to merge for us, and they have become almost a composite character in our minds.

- They do not think of themselves as old and don't talk about age.

- They know how old they are but consider it a dull subject for conversation.

- Never once during interviews did they use clichés like: "I'm not as young as I once was," "I have to slow down now," "I can't do as much as I once did," "Not at my age."

- They are vibrant and inquisitive.

- They are aware of what's happening in the world because they read and listen and care.

- They are enthusiastic about what they are doing with their lives, and, more importantly, they are interested in what *we* are doing with *ours*!

- Most appear to be in robust health, but in any case they are not obsessed with their physical conditions or subjects pertaining thereto.

- They realized far ahead that retirement was in the offing and they began planning accordingly. When the big day came, they were ready for it! Immediately they launched into a brand new course of action, allowing no time for depression or boredom to set in.

- They calculate that tomorrow is only 24 hours past today, and the chances are excellent that they won't lose any important skills (mental *or* physical) overnight. They fully expect, therefore, to be as active and productive tomorrow as they are today.

- They are impatient with all others who are wasting this phase of their lives and often employ such expressions as: "People should get motivated," "Use it or lose it," "You gotta get out of bed," "I had to do something," "Rocking is not for me," "I couldn't just sit around."

- They have a sense of humor, laugh easily, are optimistic, and don't take themselves too seriously.

- They hug a lot, display a willingness to share their favorite things with others, and give strong evidence that their relationship with God is intact.

After about 25,000 miles, we began to arrive at several unscientific but rather obvious conclusions. Example: the married couples we met were happiest when one or both of the partners were avidly into *something*. Often the husband and wife shared a common interest. However, when the husband's avocation was paramount, in every case the wife encouraged, bragged, and supported his efforts to the hilt. Likewise, when it was the wife who had a special ability, the husband was equally proud and supportive.

A second observation was that wealth and luxurious homes were emphatically *not* the features which determined a happy adjustment to the retirement experience. Even the companionship of a lifetime partner could not be regarded as an essential ingredient, judging by the fact that more than a fourth of the interviewed subjects in our book were spending their retirement years alone.

All of which points to the incontrovertible truth that *ATTITUDE* is the key ingredient in avoiding the retirement trap. The persons with the healthy psyches, the positive, forward-thinking mind-sets—those are the ones who, regardless of conditions, thumb their noses at the retirement trap as they whistle on down the road.

A variety of factors had motivated the persons we interviewed toward finding a satisfying focus for their after-career lives.

- Some of our new friends were motivated by a long cherished but unrealized *dream* they had yearned to pursue.

- Some had a persistent urge to *serve* others.

- Some sought *adventure* as an outlet for their energies.

- Some responded to the challenge of a *new career*.

- Some looked forward to expanding and enjoying an almost *full-time hobby*.

- Some revelled in the opportunity to finally express their *creativity* to its fullest extent.

- And some felt compelled to complete a worth-while project to leave as a *legacy* to the world.

Assuredly, not one of our innovative, self-starting friends was spurred to action by a single influence. But whatever their motivation, the pursuit of their dream was their very own, and it did exactly what it was intended to do: kept them out of the retirement trap—free, focused, and fulfilled!

INDEX

cross-indexed according to primary motivation

To pursue a hobby

Guion, Robert 145

Hickman,
  Goldie/Otis 153

Hopkinson, Harold 133

Knowlton, Ernie 89

To leave a legacy

Ambler, Curtis 33

Fujinaga, George 49

Kuhlman, Gus 125

Price, Ray 29

To be creative

Burt, Ruth 121

Conrad, Ruth 185

Meachen, Wini 165

McLelland, Ed 137

Robinson,
  June Elizabeth 93

Simons, Ken 69

Truslow,
  Virginia/Ted 185

Voss, Don 141